Jamaica and the United States Caribbean Basin Initiative

American University Studies

Series X
Political Science
Vol. 44

PETER LANG
New York • Washington, D.C./Baltimore • San Francisco
Bern • Frankfurt am Main • Berlin • Vienna • Paris

Clinton G. Hewan

Jamaica and the United States Caribbean Basin Initiative

Showpiece or Failure?

PETER LANG
New York • Washington, D.C./Baltimore • San Francisco
Bern • Frankfurt am Main • Berlin • Vienna • Paris

Library of Congress Cataloging-in-Publication Data

Hewan, Clinton G.
 Jamaica and the United States Caribbean Basin Initiative: showpiece or failure? / Clinton G. Hewan.
  p. cm. — (American university studies. Series X, Political science; v. 44)
 Includes bibliographical references.
 1. Jamaica—Economic policy. 2. Jamaica—Politics and government—1962– . 3. Economic assistance, American—Jamaica. 4. Caribbean Basin Initiative, 1983– I. Title. II. Series.
 HC154.H48   1994   338.97292—dc20   93-42369
 ISBN 0-8204-2345-9   CIP
 ISSN 0740-0470

Die Deutsche Bibliothek-CIP-Einheitsaufnahme

Hewan, Clinton G.:
Jamaica and the United States Caribbean basin initiative: showpiece or failure? / Clinton G. Hewan. - New York; Baltimore; San Francisco; Bern; Frankfurt am Main; Berlin; Vienna; Paris: Lang, 1994
 (American university studies: Ser. 10, Political science; Vol. 44)
 ISBN 0-8204-2345-9
NE: American university studies / 10

The paper in this book meets the guidelines for permanence and durability of the Committee on Production Guidelines for Book Longevity of the Council on Library Resources.

© Peter Lang Publishing, Inc., New York 1994

All rights reserved.
Reprint or reproduction, even partially, in all forms such as microfilm, xerography, microfiche, microcard, offset strictly prohibited.

Printed in the United States of America.

**To the Memory of
Addison Reed**

Acknowledgments

There are many people that contributed to the success of this book. First, I would like to acknowledge the editorial expertise, friendship and guidance of Dr. Norman C. Thomas. I take pride in recognizing Professor Thomas as one of my mentors. I would also like to thank Dr. Eric Weise, Professor Emeritus, and Dr. Han-Kyo Kim for their invaluable assistance. I am truly fortunate to have been allowed to stand on the shoulders of these giants.

I could not have attained the level of my accomplishment without the help and guidance of many others, namely, my colleagues at Northern Kentucky University, in particular, Dr. Addison Reed, in whose memory I dedicate this work. I would also like to thank my late mother, Emily, and father, Daniel, whose love sustained me in my formative years. My mother instilled a desire to always do my best at whatever I chose to do. I hope this project lives up to that standard.

Most importantly, I would like to thank my wife, Virginia, and daughter, Monique, for their love and assistance in all my endeavors throughout the years. I would not have accomplished what I have without their support. Finally, I wish to thank Mrs. Geri Kirchner, whose unfaltering labor of love saw to the typing and arranging of the manuscript.

Of course, any errors in this book are solely mine. If this project has merit it is due in major part to the contributions of those mentioned here.

Table of Contents

	Preface	xi
1	Introduction	1
2	Emergence of Economic Planning in Jamaica	13
3	Independence and the Changing of the Guard: 1962—1980	33
4	The State: Political and Economic Conflict	57
5	The Caribbean Basin Initiative: Genesis of the Policy	87
6	The Impact of the Caribbean Basin Initiative on the Jamaican Economy: Showpiece or Failure	113
	Bibliography	139

Preface

This study is an analysis of United States Foreign Policy in the Caribbean and Central American region in general, and Jamaica in particular with special emphasis on the Caribbean Basin Initiative. The purpose of the study is aimed at answering a number of important policy questions in regard to the impact of the CBI on the economic and socio-political conditions in the recipient countries.

Emphasis is placed on Jamaica because, far in excess of its apparent geopolitical influence, Jamaica is clearly a Caribbean nation highly placed on the list of importance with regard to United States policy in Central America and the Caribbean. Thus, the focus of my research seeks to identify and determine the extent of the success and/or failure of the Caribbean Basin Initiative, and further, to determine the geopolitical as well as strategic importance of the Caribbean Basin within the context of U.S. foreign policy, and why Jamaica was designated to play a major role in the implementation of the CBI policy objective.

Other equally important questions raised, sought answers to the role of the U.S. government in regard to the problems experienced by the Michael Manley Administration (1972-1980), and whether the U.S. government did in fact set the stage for the strong pro-U.S. role played by Edward Seaga, and the initiation of the CBI.

The works of other scholars were examined to determine what might be the possible explanations for the shift in policy by the Reagan Administration in the implementation of the CBI. Anthony Payne, Abraham Lowenthal, Deere et al, and Carl Stone among others, argue that the maintenance of U.S. hegemonic control conducive to U.S. economic and security interests and not the economic welfare of the recipient countries is the primary reason for the shift of policy.

Policy options were also examined. After an extensive discussion of the arguments of proponents and opponents of the CBI and an examination of the policy issues encountered by all parties involved, a clearer picture emerges that gives credence to the charges that U.S. national interest were paramount.

It is concluded that the primary objective of the CBI was the continuation of United States policies that evolved over time thus reflecting the Reagan Administration's heightened interest in military security, political loyalty, and advantages for U.S. economic interests.

1
Introduction

The Caribbean Basin[1] is comprised of twenty-four small developing countries situated in Central America, the Caribbean, and Northern South America. In the view of some officials in the United States, primarily those in the State Department, the region forms the third border of the United States in that it contains vital sea lanes through which three-quarters of U.S. oil imports must flow. The region is also an important market for U.S. exports with the potential for expansion.

The Caribbean Basin, Central America and all of the area known as Latin America, are considered within U.S. policy-making circles, to be inextricably tied to United States security interests. Historically, as attested to by the Monroe Doctrine (before and after its inception) this area has been defined and treated as an integral part of the sphere of influence of the United States. It should be noted in view of its importance that the Latin American continent, including South and Central America and the Caribbean, is a very large area. It encompasses some eight million square miles of land (19 percent of the world's total) and has a population of approximately 340 million people (Wiarda and Kline, 1987, p. 19).

No less a person than President Ronald Reagan stated that the Caribbean region is a "vital strategic and commercial artery for the United States. Nearly half of our trade, two-thirds of our imported oil and over half of our imported strategic materials pass through the Panama Canal or the Gulf of Mexico."[2]

Since 1981 the countries of the Caribbean Basin area have been seriously affected by the escalating cost of oil and declining prices for their major exports (bauxite, sugar and coffee, among others). Their economies, which are based on capital primarily from U.S. multinational corporations, experienced severe difficulties when these firms suffered dislocations in the 1960s and 1970s. Social and economic problems became rife in the Caribbean (Young and Phillips

1986). Quoting from the 1980 Inter-American Development Bank's statistics Young and Phillips (1986) argue that:

> Such problems were evidenced by widespread income inequality in Jamaica, Trinidad/Tobago, and Guyana. Unemployment and underemployment levels in these countries ranged from 25 to 50 percent, inflation ranged between 10 and 32 percent, and foreign exchange problems were prevalent. In the mini states of the Eastern Caribbean, where the level of industrialization and productivity is even lower, the social and political reality was even grimmer.

This crisis amplified the deep rooted structural economic problems and, in time, caused serious inflation, coupled with high unemployment, declining gross-domestic product (GDP) growth, and serious balance of payment problems. The region-states also experienced a pressing liquidity crisis which threatened the very existence of their respective economic systems.

In an effort to respond positively to the economic crisis which threatened political and social stability throughout the region, the United States in collaboration with three other regional states—Mexico, Venezuela, and Canada-announced on February 24, 1982, a joint program aimed at helping to alleviate these problems. Mexico and Venezuela agreed to help offset energy costs to the Caribbean basin countries through the implementation of a special oil facility. Canada, for its part, doubled its already significant economic assistance.

With respect to the United States, its Caribbean Basin initiative is an economic program that integrates trade, aid, and investments and represents a long-term commitment to the countries of the Caribbean and Central America. The basic aim of the program is to make use of the "magic" of the market place, the market of the Americas, to help the countries of the region to earn their own way toward self-sustaining growth.

Jamaica, one of the beneficiary-countries, and designated "showpiece" (as well as the primary focus of this study) placed great emphasis on the Caribbean Basin Initiative, mainly because the initiative policy was the creation of then Prime Minister Edward Seaga. The government of Jamaica saw in the program an opportunity to influence trade and aid patterns in the area, moving from dependence on foreign aid in the form of grants and loans, to a position of self-reliance based on joint development projects.

Purpose of the Study

Jamaica is clearly a Caribbean nation highly placed on the list of importance with regard to United States policy in the Caribbean. At the time of the CBI's enactment in 1983, it was anticipated that Jamaica would be the "showpiece" country among the CBI's beneficiaries.[3] The central purpose of this study is to identify and determine the extent of the success of the Caribbean Basin initiative, a United States policy aimed at the economic and social-development of the Caribbean and Central American nations in general and Jamaica in particular.

As one of the few Third World states in which relatively stable parliamentary government has survived after 27 years of independence, Jamaica presents an interesting case study of socio-economic politics in a developing country.[4] Jamaica's road to economic independence, it can be argued, differs very little from that experienced by other Third World nations since the end of WWII. Yet it is also true in that Jamaica's experience contains elements of uniqueness.

Jamaica, the largest of the former British West Indian Islands, is situated some 120 miles from the city of Santiago on the southeast cast of Cuba, and about 650 nautical miles south-southeast of Miami, Florida. The island is situated almost in the middle of the Caribbean Sea, historically a body of water with great political importance. Since the battle of the Saints in 1782, the only great naval battle fought in the Caribbean, there has been a continuous struggle in these waters for naval supremacy and the control of trade.[5] Jamaica has been the focal point of that conflict.

The geopolitical as well as strategic importance of the Caribbean Basin within the context of U.S. foreign policy, and the role Jamaica is expected to play and has played in the implementation of that policy objective, must be fully understood. The point should also be made that the Caribbean Basin and Central America are, within the context of United States security concerns, one geostrategic entity. This Basin is controlled from the land areas surrounding it and forms with Mexico the southern flank of the United States. The Caribbean Basin is replete with passages or choke points which are important military features.[6] These features have not escaped the notice of U.S. foreign policy makers. The Monroe Doctrine and subsequent U.S. strategic military and economic initiatives in the region attest to that fact.

Like other Third World nations, Jamaica experienced, upon receiving independence from British colonialism, enormous problems in its attempts to define and develop a strategic formula for economic development. Problems were also encountered in its attempts to chart a future course of political and social change. For most Third World states, Jamaica being no exception, the period immediately following independence from colonial rule has been most critical in setting the pattern of political, economic, and social change. This becomes evident when the restraints brought about by the scarcity of economic resource endowment and the attendant lack of adequately trained indigenous professionals, occasioned by the policies formulated and implemented by the colonial government, are examined.[7]

Similarly the inherited legacies of political institutions—a parliamentary democracy in theory, and in practice rule responsive to the elite minority only - were put to the severest of tests in an effort to cope with heightened domestic political, economic and social expectations, as well as external power contentions, primarily regional hegemonic power politics, and conflicts of interests.[8]

For Jamaica, the dynamic leadership of the country, particularly in the 1970s under Michael Manley, provided the stimulus for a move toward economic realism. Carl Stone has noted that Manley emerged as a major Third World spokesman articulating the case for a new international economic order.[9] Indeed the Manley government was quite cognizant of the dangerous decline in the country's economy brought on in part by its faulty economic policies which in turn were compounded by the oil price increases. It sought aid from the International Monetary Fund (IMF) in circumstances which, as Stone has argued, sharply posed a contradiction between a socialist-leaning regime and a conservative international lending organization. However, Manley, despite his socialist rhetoric, did not understand fully the dynamics of the interaction of Third World politics and economics and superpower considerations.

Manley's ideological approach contrasts with the pragmatism exhibited by the administration of Edward Seaga, whose Jamaica Labour Party (JLP) defeated Manley's Peoples National Party (PNP) in the general election of 1980. However, Seaga like Manley suffered similar frustrations in his attempts to develop the Jamaican economy. It is to be understood, however, that both leaders despite the articulated difference in political ideology—Michael Manley espousing a democratic socialist ideology while Edward Seaga voiced one described as capitalist conservatism—confronted the same historical and contemporary problems which largely contributed to their respective failures.

This study will demonstrate, as Stone has forcefully argued, that the stress encountered from unfulfilled expectations for rapid social and economic change fueled new elements of political opposition. The balance of power in Jamaica's domestic politics shifted in direct proportion to "powerful internal and external pressures". Jamaica's principal political leaders, beginning with Sir Alexander Bustamente, founder and leader of the Jamaica Labour Party, and Norman Washington Manley, founder and leader of the People's National Party, sought through every conceivable means to consolidate their respective power bases on the ever uncertain entities of weak economics, limited policy capabilities, and unstable political alliances. Stone argues that Jamaica is one of the English-speaking Caribbean territories in which parliamentary politics based on a competitive party system has so far survived the traumas of the post independence period.[10] This survival came about primarily because the incumbent governments encouraged institutions to adapt to the cross pressures encountered, as well as to develop new instruments of public management capable of sustaining a viable political system.

Thus Jamaica, unlike other English-speaking Caribbean countries, attempted with moderate success to utilize a number of primary government initiated functions, such as public and economic management, policy articulation, legitimacy, welfare, mobilization, security, and conflict resolution in the interest of the state.[11] The study will examine whether an overdependence on U.S. policy objectives, especially the CBI, has aggravated these post independence traumas.

Jamaica is, second to none, the Caribbean country, that as a result of its external and internal politics coupled with its strategic geographic location, has taken on an aura of importance within the context of United States hemispheric policies. This importance far surpasses Jamaica's relevance in international politics, as determined by some Jamaicans, as well as most Western European Powers.

In an effort to further an understanding of the dynamics of the Caribbean Basin Initiative, the study will also examine: the emergence of industrial planning for economic and social development in Jamaica and how this effort has been impacted by Jamaica's historical heritage; the legacy of colonialism; the attainment of independence in 1962; the political system which evolved; and, the events leading up to the general election of 1980, from which the idea for a Caribbean Basin Initiative originated with the victory of Edward Seaga and the Jamaica Labour Party.

Most importantly, this study will examine the impact of the Caribbean Basin Initiative on Jamaica's developmental strategy in terms of the objectives announced and the goals accomplished by the Reagan Administration. An analysis of the Initiative will be undertaken to identify and define the deviations from the original policy objectives. Essentially why these deviations resulted in the failure of policy objectives will be analyzed. It will be demonstrated that were it not for these deviations the Caribbean Basin Initiative could have established a precedent for U.S.-Third World economic, social and political relations.

Research Design

This study begins with a hypothesis that the Caribbean Basin Initiative may not have realized the policy objectives enunciated by the administration of Ronald Reagan (Zorn and Mayerson, 1983). This is particularly evident in the Jamaican economy through the years 1983 to 1989. It will show that the economics of the participating member states in general and Jamaica in particular registered no appreciable increase. Indeed a noticeable weakening of the economies in the region created considerable alarm both regionally as well as internationally.

After a decade (1972-1982) of falling income and exceptionally high unemployment in Jamaica, it was anticipated by the Seaga administration that the CBI program would show within five years at a minimum signs of a positive impact. The study will demonstrate that these expectations were not realized. It will be seen that the government of Jamaica, as well as other leaders of Caribbean Basin Countries, have had to borrow ever increasing amounts of foreign capital to help bolster their deteriorating economies. The Jamaican economy has only recently (1987-89) begun to manifest some signs of recovery. There are no tangible signs to substantiate the argument proposed by the United States government sources that CBI is responsible.

This research is also designed to show that even before CBI was put into effect, questions were raised as to whether CBI was a "promise or a threat". Arguments were advanced to the effect that from the list of countries designated as beneficiaries, President Reagan could choose any which had expressed a desire to be so designated; were not "Communist" (the term is not defined); and had not nationalized, broken contracts with, or otherwise discriminated against U.S. investors, without making amends (Coleman and Herring, 1985).

The political and economic problems faced by the Caribbean Basin countries require an alternative frame of reference. The basic theoretical orientation of this study derives mainly from two perspectives on the CBI policy: "Power in the Caribbean" (Stone, 1986) and "The Politics of U.S. Foreign Aid" (Guess 1987).

The former gives us a framework in which a comparative study of political economics and its impact on hegemonic power maintenance can be analyzed. Stone in elaborating this framework argues that more than in any period since World War II, United States policy-makers and the mass media have focused a search-light of attention on developments in the Caribbean and Central America. This focus he argues began in earnest with President Carter's new foreign policy thrust toward support for human rights in the region and extended to the hardline anti-communism posture of the Reagan presidency. A conjuncture of regional events, Grenada, Nicaragua and Panama are examples, also served to increase the profile of Central America and the Caribbean in U.S. foreign policy (Stone, 1980).

Guess allows us to identify the way in which the activities of U.S. foreign aid influenced the emergence and continued dominance of U.S. economic interest in the Caribbean Basin countries. Guess argues that U.S. aid in the Caribbean Basin as well as other recipient areas is very much the product of a distinctive process of American bureaucratic politics. This process he contends, relates in turn to the hybrid status of foreign aid as a component of both domestic and foreign policy (Guess, 1987).

Guess goes on to argue that U.S. foreign assistance programs in many instances follow along as a willing and most important appendage to the United States' struggles for influence in the world arena. Foreign aid within the context of hegemonic politics is characterized increasingly as a desperate policy response to coups as in the case of Grenada, counter-coups, terrorism and religious fanaticism, thus making the lines between U.S. foreign policy, foreign aid and trade activities become blurred (Guess, 1987).

The positions taken by Stone and Guess are further supported by R. B. Sutcliffe, who in his forward to Teresa Hayter's *Aid to Imperialism* (1971), wrote "There is a dying belief that aid is a form of disinterested international munificence. Those who cling to this view fly in the face of clear evidence of its role as a weapon of the foreign policy of the 'donor' countries." Sutcliffe points to the fact that "Remarkably little attempt is made to disguise this fact." For instance, he argued, "President Kennedy said in 1961 that 'foreign aid is a method by which the United States maintains a position of influence and control around the world, and sustains a good many countries which would definitely collapse, or pass into the communist bloc'" (Hayter, 1971).

The attempts by State Department strategic planning to install a new pattern of relations between the United States and the civil-societies of the respective Caribbean Basin countries suggest a new mode of articulation between the United States and the Caribbean Basin Third World. What is particularly interesting in analyzing the development of the Reagan Administration's CBI policy and the rapid development of military and para-military forces in the Eastern Caribbean mini-states is the discovery that the policy in fact strengthens the U.S. position. Also, it helps to isolate member states thus ensuring an increase in the dependency syndrome (Feinberg, 1983; Young and Phillips, 1986).

The second perspective, which sees United States policy as advocating continued regional dominance through economic controls as well as guaranteeing markets and strategic raw materials availability, will help us understand the nature and structure of U.S. Caribbean policy. Combined and carefully analyzed, the two perspectives produce a useful theoretical model for explaining the relations between politics and economics (foreign aid) as utilized by the United States in its Caribbean Basin foreign policy.

The approach to be taken here is mainly historical, complemented by a descriptive political/economic, military focus. Since the implementation of U.S. foreign policy in the Caribbean Basin defies application of a general theory, a comparative-historical approach focusing on a single country (Jamaica) and a particular policy (the CBI), will be more profitable in revealing the impact of the United States' unique foreign policy initiatives in the region.

This is also a case study of Jamaica–U.S. relations. It is designed to grasp and suggest a more accurate analysis of Jamaica's recent political/economic experiences with the United States in regard to the Caribbean Basin Initiative. The CBI was often misrepresented by State Department releases and in releases emanating from the Seaga Administration in Jamaica.

A case study can be useful in helping to arrive at a conclusion and aid in refining existing observations. The objective here will be to compare the Jamaican CBI experience with the successes claimed by the U.S. State Department and other governmental organizations.

Methodology

The method of presentation of these research findings and conclusions will involve a qualitative policy analysis of the impact and effects of the Caribbean Basin Initiative. The information sources will encompass a number of relevant government publications, news reports, and secondary analyses by journalists and scholars as well as personal interviews with high ranking government officials both in the United States and Jamaican governments. The information obtained provides the basis for evaluating the impact and subsequent effects of the CBI on the political economy of the Caribbean Basin countries in general and that of Jamaica in particular.

Among the secondary sources will be a number of publications by Carl Stone, one of Jamaica's foremost authorities on political economics. Stone's analysis of the political economy of the Caribbean in which he examines the role of United States economic policy in the region will be of primary importance. In his analysis, Stone concludes that the Caribbean Basin area "has acquired greater policy importance" with regard to the hemispheric agenda of the United States (Stone, 1985). The evidence to be presented here reinforces this conclusion.

Stone identifies three basic reasons as being responsible for the "greater policy importance" of the region; (1) the Caribbean—an area in which there are large investments of United States capital—has experienced dramatic changes in the governing coalition in some states, thereby becoming a cause for concern to the U.S.; (2) increased conflict during the 1970s between core countries in the region and the nations on the periphery; and (3) important political changes in Central America and the Caribbean during the 1970s which were contrary to U.S. interests, such as the Sandanista revolution in Nicaragua and the establishment of a Marxist-Leninist government in Grenada. These factors provide the background for and substantiate the arguments I will present regarding the political decisions underpinning U.S. aid policy in the Caribbean Basin area.

Numerous other sources will be used in explaining the lack of a viable U.S. foreign policy in the Caribbean Basin area. These sources will be utilized to help answer the questions concerning the effectiveness of the CBI. The sources give credence to George Guess' contention that "despite its historical inability" to achieve a semblance of success or "even unconditional failures", U.S. foreign aid is seen as a very controversial component of U.S. foreign policy (Guess, 1987).

Correspondingly, the conclusions I have drawn will corroborate David Bray's position that among other Caribbean countries, Jamaica is one of the major capitalist economies of the "insular Caribbean," and finds itself beset by "seemingly insoluble economic crisis." Bray points to the fact that despite a determined effort to practice a "Reaganesque policy" Jamaica's unemployment rate continues to grow excessively high, showing only a slight downturn from the highs of the first Manley period, 1972-1980 (Tardanico, 1987).

The conclusion of Jean Zorn and Harold Mayerson in their extensive analysis of the CBI—that the policy was primarily aimed at enhancing private U.S. economic interests and not that of the recipient states—will be used to show the reasons for the questionable success of the CBI. My contention that the Reagan Administration deviated from the original aims of the CBI is strongly supported by their analysis. According to Zorn and Mayerson the primary purpose of the CBI were the protection and promotion of private U.S. investments in the region and not, as the Reagan administration repeatedly argues, the enhancement of economies of the recipient countries.

My analysis supports the Zorn and Mayerson contention that the CBI program was aimed at making specific sectors of the Caribbean Basin safe for private investments in general, and for foreign investments from the United States in particular, with the expressed aim of maintaining hegemonic control over the area. This deviation in policy has resulted not in economic development for the Central American and Caribbean countries concerned, but rather in a state of dependence on the United States, increasing debt and foreign exchange burdens (Zorn and Mayerson, 1983).

Organization of the Study

This study will consist of six main parts: (1) Introduction; (2) The emergence of economic planning as a developmental strategy along with the historical heritage, and the legacy of colonialism; (3) The advent of political independence in 1962; the political system, the 1980 general election and the changing of political administrations; (4) The State: Political and economic conflict; (5) The Caribbean Basin Initiative, formulation and implementation; and (6) Jamaica and the CBI, failure of policy objective and the reasons, summary and conclusions.

In Chapter Two a theoretical framework will be developed through an examination of the emergence of industrial planning for economic development in Jamaica. The first section surveys the relevant literature on economic planning and evaluates their strengths and weakness in explaining the impact of economic planning on the Jamaican economy. The second section seeks to explain the impact of Jamaica's historical heritage as well as the legacy of colonialism on the political and economic development of the island.

In Chapter Three, an analysis of the political culture of Jamaica as well as the political and economic conflicts experienced will be undertaken. Chapter Four will examine the Jamaican state as well as the political and economic conflicts experienced after 1962. Chapter Five will analyze the Caribbean Basin Initiative, from the standpoint of the formulation and implementation of the policy. The reasons underpinning the failure of the initiative will be examined in light of policy changes emanating from Washington D.C. Finally, in Chapter Six conclusions and findings will be discussed with regard to the political, economic and social impact of the initiative on the Jamaican economy.

Notes

1. "Caribbean Basin" refers to the region known as the Caribbean Sea, bordered on the north by Cuba, Jamaica, Haiti, Dominican Republic and Puerto Rico, on the east by Leeward and Windward Islands, on the west by Mexico and on the south by Central America.

2. "The Gulf of Mexico" in this study refers to the body of water northwest of the Caribbean Sea bordered on the north, west and southwest by the United States and Mexico, and the east by Cuba.

3. "CBI beneficiaries" refers to the 21 countries which qualify, as of September 1988, which have fulfilled the requirements stipulated in the Caribbean Basin Economic Recovery Act, enacted into law August 5, 1983 and made effective January 1, 1984. Six additional countries potentially are eligible for CBI trade benefits but, with the exception of Guyana, have not formally requested designation.

4. The growth and impact of socio-economic politics in Jamaica will be shown to present a unique case study of the major social and political features of the contention for power in Jamaica's domestic political arena.

5. Int. Security Council (CAUSA INT.), Page 1, (1985).

6. U.S. Department of Commerce (FET 87-102), Int. Marketing Series, U.S. Embassy, Kingston, Jamaica, (1987).

7. Stone, Carl, *Democracy and Clientelism in Jamaica*, Page 71, (1980).

8. Stone, Carl, *Democracy and Clientelism in Jamaica*, p. 71, (1980).

9. Michael Manley's emergence as a spokesman for the new international economic order, refers to the leadership (both regional and international) given by Michael Manley from 1973 to the present in articulating the need for a restructuring of the International economic system.

10. Stone, Carl, *Democracy and Clientelism in Jamaica* (1980).

11. Burns, Sir Allan, *History of the British West Indies*, (1954).

2
Emergence of Economic Planning in Jamaica

Jamaica, like most Third World countries, recognized the importance of pursuing a policy of economic development conducive to the maintenance of a viable and productive society. It is with this very vital aspect of national development firmly in mind that the newly emerging independent government took over the reins of governmental control in 1962. The emergence of industrial planning aimed at economic development did not, however, start with the granting of political independence by the British colonial powers. Strident political as well as economic voices emanating from Jamaican leaders such as Dr. Robert Love, JAG Smith, Marcus Garvey, Alexander Bustamante and Norman Washington Manley gave testimony to the fact that there were those who were very cognizant of the need for such planning. They began the task—to some analysts, the dream—from the early period of internal self government, which served as a training ground for eventual political independence.

Historically, as customary in colonial servitude, early planning for economic development rests primarily in the domain of the colonial powers, the aim of which was more toward satisfying the profit margins of the expatriate entrepreneurs rather than enhancing the economic opportunities of the native peoples. Jamaica having similar experiences as other colonial enclaves had very little involvement in the earlier stages of its industrial planning. This was done primarily by the British, and was carefully structured to supply needed raw material for British and European manufacturing concerns as well as their markets. This type of industrial planning sought not to develop the indigenous economies in terms of benefiting the natives, but rather to enhance their capacity for producing a variety of materials and semi-finished products conducive to the development of British home-based industries.

The history and the political economy of every country in the modern world has been influenced to some degree by its association with some other country or countries whose technological status happened to be somewhat more advanced. The history and political economy of Jamaica proved no exception to this rule. Apart from its exposure to foreign cultures, other important factors such as the colonial experience, slavery, an agriculture based economy and the absentee landlord system also influenced the emergence of industrial planning in Jamaica.

Jamaica is the largest of the former British West Indian islands and is situated approximately 120 miles from the city of Santiago on the southeast coast of Cuba and about 600 miles from the city of Barranqulla on the northwest coast of Columbia. The island covers an area 4,411 square miles, almost the size of the state of Connecticut. The island's land mass is very irregular with less than 25% of the land area considered flat, while more than 8% is seen as unsuitable for agricultural purposes. Jamaica's major natural resource consists of more than 1.5 billion tons of bauxite the major exploitation of which, up to the late 1970's, was controlled exclusively by foreign interests.

Jamaica is virtually lacking in any form of energy resource. Except for a few small "experimental" hydro electric facilities, all domestic energy consumption is based on imported oil. In the early stages of the island's development coal, also imported, was widely used. From its early colonial days, first by the Spanish beginning in 1492 and subsequently by the British who took over in 1655, Jamaica was utilized as a producer of primary products. Gayle points to the fact that as a British colony for three centuries, Jamaica produced primary products for export to the metropolitan country and imported the entire range of consumer goods (Gayle, 1986, p. 131).

The British colonial policy practiced throughout the period dictated a scenario whereby economic activity was primarily limited to the distribution of imported goods. Indeed even when, as Gayle argues, a range of locally manufactured alternatives became available, the consumption of foreign goods represented a status symbol irrespective of price and quality comparisons (Gayle, p. 131).

The exploitation of the resources of Jamaica has, it can be argued, involved very large supplies of the mobile factors of production. These factors were introduced from overseas and their history is well known. Cumper argues that "Capital, too, has been imported in many forms, supplied usually by the merchants who traded in West India produce" (Cumper,1974, p. 2). While Cumper dealt with the West Indies in general, his observations regarding the economic development of the region also provide the basis for an analysis of Jamaica in particular.

As in other areas of the West Indies, Jamaica benefited from the importation of capital in many forms, such as loans and direct development investment. Indeed Cumper points to the fact that the immigrants who went to the West Indies brought with them a wide variety of specialized skills along with needed managerial ability (Cumper, 1974). Yet to argue that economic development in the Caribbean in general, or Jamaica in particular, is a reflection only of the region's interaction with Britain and other metropolitan powers is very misleading. From a relatively early period, Cumper argues, the area contributed substantially toward its own economic advancement.

In the area of capital formation the contribution of Jamaica to its economic development, as was the case of other Caribbean countries, was by no means negligible. Cumper argues that this contribution cannot be adequately measured primarily in view of the fact that such contribution took the form of a direct application of labor to investment (Cumper, 1974, p. 3).

In Jamaica, as in other Caribbean countries, the application of labor consisted of the clearing of land, the building of roads, buildings and other fixed capital all produced by the slaves themselves. Indeed it can be argued the West Indies evolved their own dynamic system of agricultural management techniques with respect to plantations as well as other crops. The preoccupation with the relations of the West Indies to the metropolitan powers also affected economic development in other ways, principally the exaggeration of the role of production for export in the economy.

British colonial policy, Cumper argues, was long based on the assumption that only the export trade was of importance. Yet the authors of the *Jamaican Almanac* for the year 1839, in estimating the value of "property annually created or prepared" in the island set down the value of all exports at only $2.5 million while domestic manufacturers were put at $2 million and the production of vegetable food at $1.2 million (Cumper, 1974, p. 4). Although, the figures given may have been inaccurate, contemporaries did not find them improbable. Jamaica may have indeed produced a lot more of its own food than some other Caribbean countries.

The Role of Agriculture in Early Economic Planning

With the attainment of independence from British colonial rule, Jamaica began to place more emphasis upon industrialization. Planning for industrial sector development became even more important in light of the fact that the agriculture based economy has been stigmatized with a colonial status. Indeed in Jamaica as well as in other West Indian territories, sugar and exploitation have been almost synonymous (Mathews and Andic, 1971). In an analysis of politics and economics in the Caribbean, Mathews observed that Trinidad and Guyana began to develop their mineral resources in the post-world war period. However, Jamaica which started mining bauxite much later, discussed plans for a nuclear power plant which would allow the intermediate step of converting bauxite into alumina. Mathews argued that the Canadian Aluminum Company (ALCAN) operating in Jamaica had already taken that step in its operations. He added, however, that the three American firms (Reynolds, Alcoa, and Revere) were reluctant to adopt similar procedures since it was thought that they would risk provoking a suspended United States Tariff on alumina. Mathews concluded that a nuclear power plant would make the case too strong to resist and thus provide more industrial jobs for Jamaicans (Mathews and Andic, 1971, p. 274).

Those who opposed the seemingly heavy emphasis on industrial development in the early planning stages argued that such a policy neglected agriculture which had been at the base of the Jamaican economic structure. In contrast proponents of a rapid industrialization policy argued that despite the unbalanced attention given to industrial development in preference to agriculture, it is in the area of industry that some immediate economic improvements have been observed. Jamaica has registered growing trade deficits since independence, which in itself is not too alarming. But as Mathews argues when a sizeable portion of foreign spending is aimed at securing the commodities necessary for sustaining life (such as foodstuffs) for an island with an important agricultural enterprise, then there is cause for alarm (Mathews and Andic, 1971, p. 248).

It can be argued with some justification that planning for industrial development in Jamaica presented a seemingly insurmountable task, primarily as a result of the economic situation inherited from the colonial period. Planners were faced with the challenge of overcoming or at least mitigating these situations which, as Michael Manley pointed out, displayed eight basic characteristics. These Manley described as export-import orientation; the trader mentality; lack of confidence; the absence of linkages; poverty and value added; foreign capital and foreign technology; irrelevant education; and the gap between the rich and the poor.[1]

The overemphasis placed on industrial development primarily after World War II adversely affected agricultural growth in Jamaica. While it must have been obvious to economic planners at the time that a strong agricultural base was essential, this thought was never translated into reality. Agriculture, which should have developed simultaneously with industry, lagged far behind it. This compounded and adversely impacted upon the general state of the economy and rendered the economy incapable of distributing benefits equitably. Manly argues that the failure to mount an assault upon the problem of agriculture, particularly in view of the fact that some 24% of the working population depended directly upon the land, was to prove disastrous in later years. Indeed he argued, it is in the failure of agriculture that is to be found a primary cause of the gap existing between the haves and the have-nots in Jamaican society (Manley, 1975).

The neglect of agriculture in developmental planning in Jamaica and the entire Caribbean region is regarded by Ransford W. Palmer, "as partly founded on the premise, that in capital-scarce countries, the allocation of capital should be toward the development of that sector which promises the highest rate of return" (Palmer, 1984, p. 17). Unfortunately, planning for industrial development was in essence a strategy aimed at the rapid accumulation of scarce capital primarily from two very important sources; external as well as expected high profits generated internally. As has been demonstrated over the decades, a less profitable agricultural sector of the economy fell far behind and was in no position, as Palmer argues, "to compete with industry for scarce capital" (Palmer 1984).

Economic planners in Jamaica confronted the problem of resource allocation impacting upon industrialization as well as agricultural development. Similar to other Caribbean areas, the task was made more difficult in Jamaica due to the seemingly unending migration from rural areas to the towns and cities. This migration presented planners with two fundamental problems. On the one hand, workers previously engaged in agricultural production were no longer available in adequate numbers thereby further aggravating an already precarious situation. On the other hand, the resulting overpopulation and unemployment in the towns and cities, taxed to the limit the scarce financial resources available.

W. Arthur Lewis, in an analysis of the impact of population relocation in developing countries, points to the fact that dependence upon adequate finances by developing countries results directly from unusually high population growth rates in urban areas (Lewis, 1978). Palmer argues, however, that while urbanization has in fact increased the need for external capital, a problem arises if this urbanization is viewed in "isolation from the industrial process." Palmer further argues that "while high population growth rates in the rural areas push people off the farms, urban industrial development pulls them into the cities. Thus, one could argue that industrialization intensifies financial dependence" (Palmer, 1984, p. 17).

The Role of Industrialization in Jamaica's Economic Planning

Jamaica, like other countries in the Caribbean region, experienced the growth pains associated with the transition from an agriculturally based economy to one based on industry. This transition followed the classic pattern whereby industrialization proceeded at the expense of agricultural development. Palmer points to the fact that industrialization in the Caribbean has been based on a strategy of import substitution. He further argues that the neglect of agriculture is partly founded on the premise that in capital-scarce countries, the allocation of capital should be toward the development of the sector which promises the highest rate of return (Palmer, 1984, p. 17).

The rapidity in the growth of these areas occasioned a widening gap between actual savings and required savings. Planners were forced to accept the fact that the pace of industrialization had to be accelerated in order to satisfy rising expectations and increased levels of consumption. This problem over successive years was compounded by unusually sharp increases in the price of vital imports thereby intensifying the demand for more foreign capital.

The problems confronted by Jamaica in particular and the Caribbean countries in general in their attempt to establish a viable form of development were exacerbated by the fact that their earlier existence as settler colonies represented a deliberate policy to create what Franklin W. Knight described as "miniatures of the metropolis, with a definite symbiotic relationship" (Knight, 1978, p. 122). The colonists from the very start intended to occupy and settle the land and to produce in abundance whatever the land yielded. The colony, "became their *Patrica Chica*," in reality the region to which they owed allegiance as long as it served their plans and with which they forged what passed as an identity however temporary (Knight, 1978, pp. 17-18).

Knight, as do Mathews, Palmer and Manley in their respective analyses, argues that the overriding preoccupation with the desire to exploit on the part of the settlers created a situation whereby the colonies became the center for the organization of labor and the establishment of a community geared to the maximum production of tropical staples, both for the imperial and the international markets. The question of national allegiance on the part of the Europeans was non-existent. Residence in their estimation was viewed as temporary and the European settler society in its entirety as merely a transient political and economic extension of the metropolis. Hence, they cultivated little or no feeling of identity or community of interest (Knight, 1978).

Knight explains further that the two aims of settlement and exploitation were neither clearly articulated or distinctly separated at any time. One or the other consideration superseded, or the two simply coexisted uneasily, as was evident in Curacao in the eighteenth century and in Cuba and Puerto Rico during the nineteenth century (Knight, 1978, p. 123).

Thus, it is not difficult to determine the fundamental aims of the ruling European entrepreneurial class with respect to the economic policies pursued in Jamaica. Emphasis was placed primarily on an agriculture based economy. Industrialization was reserved exclusively for the use of the "Homeland" metropolis whose finished goods manufactured from the raw materials produced by the colonies would find a ready market in the colonies at greatly inflated prices. It is to be understood that a deliberate but unsuccessful attempt was undertaken to inculcate in the minds as well as the social perception of Jamaicans, that the finished products imported from the metropolis were in essence vastly superior to those produced at home. Thus, what could be termed a vicious circle of raw material exports and finished goods imports plagued Jamaica and its attempts at industrialization from the early colonial days to the present.

Jefferson points to the fact that economic planning by the colonials during the pre-World War II period failed to deal adequately with a number of readily recognizable problems, the most important of which was population growth. This laid the foundation for the problems of chronic unemployment and underemployment which were to follow. Jefferson argues that this problem continues to plague Jamaica to the present (Jefferson, 1972, p. 3). Attempts were made to explain away this deliberate act of not taking into serious consideration the potential impact of the population explosion on the available cultivable area. Jefferson argues, however, that "Between 1870 and 1930 the average annual rate of population growth was only 1.2 per cent." Interestingly, he contends that "toward the close of the century even this modest increase was more than could be accommodated in agriculture as then organized" (Jefferson, 1972, p. 3).

Jamaica, therefore, experienced several negatives with regard to the fundamental structure of its economic base and as such entered both the pre and post second world war periods with a decided disadvantage in regard to a credible economic and financial base. Political economists as well as other observers of Jamaica's socio-political phenomena expressed at a very early date fears with regard to the possible adverse effect a rapidly expanding population may have on the economy. Indeed Jamaica's population was a mere 1.8 million when the expression of these fears first emerged.[2] The island's population has since reached, in relative density terms, a staggering 2.5 million. However, taking into account average income levels and the distribution of available income, the population is quite small. This is a vital factor especially when viewed within the context of the available technology and the consumer taste preference patterns characteristic of a market of the size and density required for sustaining the division of labor which is essential to a developed economy.

One can argue that within the context of an international situation where trade barriers have become prevalent, the proposed road to economic development on the often articulated basis of "going it alone" must in the final analysis be seen as difficult.[3] For instance the difficulty experienced in attempting to expand the land available for cultivation clashed with the need for fewer people on lands already under cultivation. It is, therefore, not surprising as Jefferson noted, that the portion of that segment of the population classified as engaged in agriculture "fell from 67 percent in 1880 to 54 percent in 1930" (Jefferson, 1972).

Aspects of Economic Planning

The 1930's proved to be the watershed years for Jamaica in the island's attempt to grapple with growing economic distress. The downward trend in the price for exports was exacerbated by the deep depression then being experienced in the industrialized countries. The real value of exports, as Jefferson noted declined during the period 1929 to 1934. The problem was further aggravated in that production for the domestic market did not expand sufficiently to arrest the evident fall in real income per capita during the above mentioned five-year period. Real income per capita gave the appearance of a slight recovery after 1935, however, this was accompanied by increasing unemployment especially when outlets for immigration to Cuba and Panama no longer existed. It was observed that the excess of labor supply had an adverse effect on wages in some sectors (Jefferson, 1972).

As a consequence of these adverse economic situations Jamaica experienced serious social disturbances beginning in May 1939. These disturbances, which quickly spread throughout the island, aggravated even further the crippling economic malaise. Similar disturbances were occurring simultaneously throughout the West Indies. Some of these began as early as 1934 in protest against prevailing economic conditions (Lewis, 1968). Jefferson noted that the Moyne Commission, which was sent by the British Government to determine the causes of the riots, reported that the disturbances resulted from the very low wages paid workers as well as the high levels of unemployment evident at the time. The Moyne Commission in attempting to help alleviate the problems, made a number of recommendations. Among these were the removal of legal and other obstacles which prevented the development of a viable trade union system and the establishment of a welfare fund geared to providing urgently needed social services. Unfortunately, the Moyne Commission's recommendations fell far short of addressing the real problems especially in regard to the long term (Jefferson, 1972, p. 4).

In keeping with the accepted policy enunciated by the colonial administration, the Moyne Commission steered clear of the issue regarding any form of an industrial development policy for Jamaica. Whatever aspect of this vital issue the Commission reluctantly confronted was hidden behind questions of tariff barriers, with a stern warning against conducting or financing "speculative industrial enterprises". Jefferson noted that the Commissions's recommendations clearly indicated its disapproval of any attempt on the part of the colonial government to pursue an active industrial development policy in Jamaica or any other area within the West Indies.

Indeed the Moyne Commission clearly demonstrated an attitude of ambivalence with respect to the role of government in efforts to encourage economic development in the British West Indies. With this sort of confusion and official neglect forming the backdrop, Jamaica moved to the next stage in its attempt at industrial development. This new stage began with the introduction of a series of reports in 1945 by two very important entities; the Economic Policy Committee and the Agricultural Policy Committee. Fearing a resurgence of the 1938 disturbances because of worsening economic and social conditions, the colonial administration, on the recommendation of the Representative Assembly, created these two bodies and charged them with the responsibility of reporting back to it. Both of these groups focused on the problems of economic development. The Economic Policy Committee concerned itself with the formulation of policies conducive to the improvement of the existing standard of living. The Agricultural Policy Committee undertook the task of devising plans aimed at the development of agriculture. The basic aim of both committees was the enhancement of employment opportunities.

Unfortunately, in keeping with established policy aims of the colonial era, the Economic Policy Committee failed to formulate a coordinated program of economic development, thus falling short of its stated objectives as did its predecessor the Moyne Commission. Reflecting the prevailing train of thought, the committee agreed that the inordinately high level of unemployment in Jamaica at the time resulted from an exorbitant price level, which the committee considered too high in comparison to other countries. The committee argued that "spectacular wage increases which had made labor costs in Jamaica the highest in the world" were primarily responsible for the economic dilemma. Referring to the 1945 Report of the Economic Policy Committee, Jefferson noted that "higher labor costs were said to check the expansion of exports, to cause local products to be replaced by imports and to prejudice the development of a construction industry, which was such a potentially large field for employment" (Jefferson, 1972, p. 6).

The message the Economic Policy Committee sought to convey, without the least bit of credible evidence, is that a combination of trade union agitation and almost nonexistent wage legislation after 1938 resulted in wages outstripping production in key sectors of the economy. Interestingly, despite that conclusion, the committee offered no suggestions for solving the problem. It did, as Jefferson noted, vaguely mention the possibility of reducing wages, which in turn hopefully would reduce the price level. The idea, however, was abandoned in view of an expected hostile reaction from the workers. One critical area in which the committee registered a negative position was with regard to a "policy of industrialization behind tariff barriers". It was argued that implementing such a policy would have an adverse effect on the cost of living.

Many prominent West Indian political economists disputed the position taken by the Economic Policy Committee. Most noted among them was Arthur Lewis who charged that the committee exhibited "a strong prejudice against the development of local industries".[4] Lewis pointed to the fact that money costs are in essence not an adequate reflection of real costs within a situation of chronic unemployment. Rather, he argued, the most practical answer for increasing employment would involve a deliberate restriction of imports while concentrating on an attempt to increase production for home consumption. Lewis argued unapologetically, that "it is clear as daylight that only a great increase in secondary industry can solve Jamaica's unemployment problems". He further maintained that it was essential that attention be concentrated on industries engaged in the processing of local material and on those whose requirements in terms of power, capital equipment, heavy raw materials and specialized skills are by comparison small and as such are not associated with marked internal economies of scale, (Lewis, 1944).

1944: Political and Constitutional Changes

In terms of fundamental impact and importance, 1944, the year in which major political and constitutional changes came to Jamaica, must be judged as second only to 1962 when political independence was finally achieved. In essence 1944 marked the beginning of a period in which a number of decisive policy initiatives by the colonial government signalled for the first time an indication that Britain intended to begin the process of relinquishing its control over the political and economic affairs of Jamaica. Some of the policy initiatives included the replacement of the Crown Colony form of government with a representative assembly which ultimately assumed a major portion of responsibility for Jamaica's internal affairs. This representative assembly was to be elected by the people under the theory of "Home Rule". Indigenous political parties were also allowed. The political parties working in conjunction with the Representative Assembly immediately began to focus their energies on plans for the island's economic development.

Owen Jefferson in his classic text, *The Post-War Economic Development of Jamaica*, noted that it became very clear from the inception of these political parties that an over reliance on market forces could not bring about a viable economic development process and that such reliance could result in disaster. Jefferson also noted that with respect to existing world-wide economic trends, government would have to become more aggressively involved in economic policy formulation—than it had in the past (Jefferson, 1972, p. 7). Regrettably, however, the system of government that emerged, although structurally different from the Crown Colony format, remained the same from the standpoint of policy formulation and content. Internal Self-Government as the new political system was formally termed, could do very little to change fundamentally existing ideas and policies regarding economic development planning. It should be understood that in 1944, while Jamaicans were allowed the freedom of exercising their voting franchise, that freedom was never intended to extend into the realm of decisive economic planning or the relevant decision making process.

In 1944, notwithstanding internal self-government, important economic planning decisions continued to be made at the Colonial Office in Whitehall. Very little attention, if any, was given to important economic planning suggestions emanating from the local elected representatives. To the Colonial Office, Jamaica was for the foreseeable future to remain first and foremost a producer of raw materials and an agriculture based economy. It can be argued that the idea of a serious approach to economic planning involving industrialization did not find a place of prominence in the thinking of the colonialists. Therefore, it should not be too difficult to identify this period as one of the early periods marking the beginning of Jamaica's perennial economic problem. The foregoing, however, is not to suggest that some semblance of an economic plan did not exist. The Colonial Government was very cognizant of the fact that it would have to play a more positive role in this regard than had been the case in the past. Jefferson addresses this issue in pointing to the fact that the need for some sort of "planning" eventually became evident.

With respect to the Caribbean in general and Jamaica in particular, the form and content of the development plans enunciated have predictably reflected to some degree the ideological orientation of the framers. The plans available to those charged with this responsibility in 1944 differ little in range and scope from those available today. Fundamentally, they range from public expenditure programs with unclear general economic goals and policy proposals to plans for the creation of a total "state economy." Economists and policy planners recognize the fact that the area between these extremes allows much room for different approaches.

Jefferson in exploring the alternatives available, points to the fact that the amount of resources utilized by the productive sector which is under the direct control of the government is of paramount importance in helping to arrive at a rational determination in regard to the direction the planning will take. Jefferson also points out that as is the case in socialist states, control of all or a greater portion of the productive resources is within the jurisdiction of the state, thus the channeling of resources can be undertaken as determined by the political directorate.

In the case of Jamaica the economic planners, beginning in 1944, confronted a choice between two major approaches: The first a near state monopoly approximating the socialist system of central planning with the productive resources under the control of the state (the system some economists consider more conducive to underdeveloped economies); and the second a system in which the productive resources are placed entirely in the hands of the private sector.

Governments between the years 1944 and 1962 chose the latter approach. This has held true also for successive governments in independent Jamaica from 1962 to the present, with the exception of the last four years of the Michael Manley administration from 1976 to 1980. (The 1972-1980 Manley administration will be dealt with in a later chapter). The latter approach, called the "Inducement Approach," entails the implementation of a number of relatively broad policy goals, the provision by government of certain incentives, and a heavy reliance on private enterprise to propel the economy forward. Fortunately, at least from the planning perspective, the planners in Jamaica have been aware of the difficulties inherent in a private sector controlled economy.

Despite the inherent difficulties which confronted the original planners of Jamaica's economic future, there was never any tangible evidence to indicate that those charged with the responsibility of guiding the island's economic progress were under any delusions as to the path they would pursue. Indeed, the belief in progress was at the very basis of the themes of what has been described as the "Democratic Revolution", which to some analysts began in general prior to the late 1930. Wendell Bell's topical reference to the "Conscious Direction of the Polity, Economy, and Society" as the conscious preoccupation of the "new indigenous elite" refers eloquently to the role of the economic planners of the late 1930s as it did for those charged with that responsibility in the 1960s.[5]

A basic inherent problem confronting those charged with the difficult task of planning for socio-economic development in Jamaica in the 1930s, centered around the fact that any accepted standard of measurement of the Jamaican economy in the early post-war period was essentially agricultural. However, since the late 1930s the relative importance of agriculture in the economic life of Jamaica has declined significantly (Eisner, 1961, p. 120). It should be remembered that in the 1930s agriculture accounted for upwards of 40% of the island's gross domestic product (GDP). Despite the dramatic decline agriculture can still be classified as forming one of the bases of the economy. Agriculture accounted for some 31% of the island's total product in 1951. In addition the supply of raw materials to industry in which agriculture plays a large part increases its contribution to almost 70 percent of recorded secondary industry output. As reported by the International Bank of Reconstruction and Development, at the beginning of the 1950s some 75% of the basic activities in the island related directly to agriculture (Jefferson, 1972, p. 75).

The rapid growth of the mining sector, which up to the early 1950s impacted minimally on the Jamaican economy, coupled with the manufacturing sector, exercised a beneficial effect on the service industries. These combined helped to decrease the share of agriculture in the island's total production. By 1968 agriculture accounted for only 10.2% of gross domestic product. Jefferson, in analyzing the overall impact of agriculture on the Jamaican economy, argued that in the area of exports agricultural products declined to approximately 35% of visible exports and to the level of 18% in the case of all exports of goods and services. He adds, however, that the census of 1960 indicated that agriculture still accounted for about 39% of the employed labor force.

It is safe to argue, therefore, that some of the basic features of the trends described above should not seem surprising. Indeed the historical experience of the West Indies as well as other formally colonial or colonized areas has demonstrated that the accepted avenue of economic development usually involves some increase in the proportion of the overall national product not connected to agriculture. Notably, a rise in per capita output shows a corresponding decrease in agricultural output, or at least a slowing down in this sector, while the output of industry and other non-agricultural sectors of the economy tend to accelerate in regard to overall output.

It is important to note, therefore, that the conditions of the 1930s that led to the riots brought home to the colonialists the grim realization that the economic and social conditions existing at the time were not conducive to a politically stable and economically healthy environment. Efforts had to be made towards a more diversified economic system, one that would endeavor to address the inequities prevalent in the society. One fact that became apparent immediately was that continued reliance on agriculture would not within the existing economic structure be able to add significantly to the changes in the economic and social system deemed necessary. As stated earlier, the Moyne Commission in its report regarding the causes of the 1939 riots, did very little to recommend tangible solutions to the problem. Thus, one can argue that the problems encountered in the post-war years found their roots in the lack of serious economic planning in the colonial era.

The Role of the Mining Industry

Because of the weakness of agriculture in the years prior to and after World War II, planners with an eye toward Jamaican political independence had to consider other sectors in which the island's economy could be invigorated. Thus, mining and light industrial manufacturing began to emerge as an alternative, or as Eisner argued, a means of diversifying the socio-economic development structure (Eisner, 1961). Mining of Jamaica's mineral resources, primarily bauxite, was minimal until the early 1960s. Both Guyana in the case of bauxite and Trinidad in the case of oil were by the 1950s further along than Jamaica in the effective exploitation of their mineral resources. Colonialism, however, weighed heavily on the mining sector, in that the original exploration and subsequent extraction contracts were handled exclusively by the colonial government.

For a considerable period of time before the second World War deposits of certain minerals were known to exist in Jamaica. Among these were low grade coal, gypsum in relatively large supply, low grade iron ore (considered not economically feasible for exploitation), and large deposits of high grade, easily mined bauxite. Of all these, including minimal reserves of other minerals, only bauxite and gypsum were considered economically feasible for exploitation. It is important, however, to understand that politics as well as physical location affects the economic potentialities of resources. The West Indies are situated in a hemisphere dominated by the United States, whose strategic, commercial and ideological policies have, whether the countries affected like it or not, influenced resource development and use. The strategic location of the Eastern Caribbean Islands resulted in the construction of United States military bases during World War II. Furthermore, the importance of the Panama Canal to United States interests has been substantially increased by the political independence and economic self-reliance movements evident in the region.

Immediate circumstances notwithstanding, economic planners in Jamaica as well as the Caribbean at large were cognizant of the concerns of hemispheric harmony. They were also aware that the ties of a common language and a common legal-political tradition indicate that whatever Caribbean economic connections with Britain were lost after political independence, these would most certainly be replaced by economic links with the United States and Canada. Cumper argues that the foregoing had two vital implications for resource development. First, that the Caribbean would be flooded with technical advice and assistance from persons "unfamiliar—as previously—with tropical ecology."
And secondly the area would continue to have "assured export markets for high-value plantation commodities" (Cumper, 1974, p. 52).

It is within this context that natural resource extraction began to play a significant role in industrial development plans for Jamaica. Important as agriculture may be (despite its declining impact), the systematic exploitation of minerals and other raw materials represented the best hope for expanding general productivity and raising living standards in the island. While bauxite would eventually come to dominate the non-agricultural economy of Jamaica, its existence was not recognized before 1942. Extraction of bauxite ore actually started ten years later in 1952. There have been questions asked as to whether those involved in negotiating the contracts with the respective mining companies did so with Jamaica's best interests at heart. Several political economists, foremost among them Jamaica's own Norman Girvan, have argued that this was not the case (Girvan, 1976).

Nevertheless, as it turned out, the mining of bauxite became a fundamental part of the industrial development plans of Jamaica. It was argued that the island was in a unique position to benefit from its vast resources of bauxite and as such should have been the primary beneficiary. However, Girvan points to the fact that the balance of power in the negotiation relationship rests heavily with the aluminum companies over most of the life of the industry. This he argues, is as true for Jamaica as it is for the entire Caribbean. The Jamaican economy as well as that of the Caribbean was, Girvan further argues, unable to benefit fully from bauxite, due in part to the overall political economic framework within which the company-state relationship has unfolded-a framework characterized by the subordination of Caribbean economic development to European and American commercial interests. He points to the fact that Jamaica, as well as other Caribbean Bauxite producers such as Surinam and Guyana, were all colonies of European powers at the time the U.S. companies first secured concessions to exploit their bauxite (Girvan, 1976, p. 110). Consequently the Caribbean bauxite producing countries, in spite of possessing the largest deposits of bauxite in the world, have found themselves confined to the simple low-value activities of the industry, specifically the extraction of the bauxite ore. Thus, as Girvan forcefully argues, the region while accounting for 38% of total world bauxite production, realizes only 16% of alumina production and a very insignificant 0.5% of world primary aluminum production (Girvan, 1976, pp. 101-103) (See Table 2).

Britain accepted de facto U.S. domination of Jamaican bauxite mining, which adversely affected the island's benefiting from this resource. Richard Reynolds, former President of Reynolds Metals, gave credence to the foregoing when he stated "it can be demonstrated that almost 20,000 jobs at Reynolds in the United States—two thirds of our total—work with bauxite, alumina or aluminum derived from Jamaica. Since the U. S. aluminum industry as a whole employs some 300,000 people and since half of the domestic industries bauxite comes from Jamaica—we are talking about 150,000 jobs in this country that trace back to raw materials from Jamaica" (Girvan, 1976, p. 98). Moreover as Girvan noted, the bauxite industry, "geared as it is to" Canada and particularly the United States, was regarded by the British as a ready and necessary dollar earner. This was particularly fortuitous since in the period during and after World War II, the British were starved for dollars needed to fight the war and to keep their ravaged economy afloat afterward. The earnings from the exploitation of bauxite in Jamaica therefore, did not go toward the economic development of the island but rather to fatten British coffers. This retarded even further any economic progress that could have been made by Jamaica prior to attaining independence.

Jamaica, indeed, (as was the case of the other Caribbean bauxite producing countries) found itself at a disadvantage in regard to the aluminum companies at a very early date. Quite evident was the fact that these companies were in a superior bargaining position. They had in their possession superior financial resources, and as Girvan noted "each of the four larger companies has a

TABLE 2 World Production of Bauxite, Alumina, and Aluminum, 1972[a]

	Bauxite		Alumina		Aluminum	
	Thousand tons	% world total	Thousand tons	% world total	Thousand tons	% world total
Jamaica	14,318	19.0	3,297	10.5	-	-
Surinam	8,573	11.4	1,323	4.1	58	0.5
Guyana	4,108	5.4	385	1.2	-	-
Dominican Republic	1,142	1.5	-	-	-	-
Haiti	863	1.1	-	-	-	-
Total Caribbean	29,004	38.4	5,005	15.9	58	0.5
Australia	15,910	21.1	3,894	12.4	227	1.8
Guinea	3,000	4.0	772	2.5	-	-
Yugoslavia	2,421	3.2	374	1.2	80	0.6
Sierra Leone	765	1.0	-	-	-	-
Ghana	349	0.5	-	-	146	1.2
Total IBA Countries	51,449	68.2	10,045	32.0	511	4.1
France	3,591	4.8	1,340	4.3	434	3.5
Greece	2,978	3.9	529	1.7	143	1.1
United States	2,125	2.8	7,760	24.7	4,122	32.9
India	1,829	2.4	453	1.4	196	1.6
Indonesia	1,407	1.9	-	-	-	-
Malaya	1,187	1.6	-	-	-	-
Brazil	550	0.7	231	0.7	107	0.9
Other Western Europe	-	-	2,215	7.1	2,070	16.5
Canada	-	-	1,387	4.4	1,000	8.0
Japan	-	-	2,638	8.4	1,119	8.9
Others	123	-	84	0.3	225	2.0
Total capitalist World	65,239	86.5	26,682	85.1	9,957	79.4
USSR	6,300	8.3	3,300	10.5	1,980	15.8
Other Eastern Europe	3,399	4.5	1,036	3.3	434	3.5
China	500	0.7	330	1.1	170	1.3
Total socialist world	10,199	13.5	4,666	14.9	2,584	20.6
World total	75,438	100.0	31,348	100.0	12,541	100.0

Sources: American Bureau of Metal Statistics and U. S. Bureau of Mines.
a. Bauxite and aluminum: production in short tons (2,000 lb); alumina: capacity in short tons.

turnover greater than the national income of the largest producing country". The superior financial resources of the companies along with their ability to demand concessions from the British and their monopoly of knowledge and information needed to establish mining operations enabled them to dominate the negotiating process.

This advantageous position, which the bauxite companies exploited to the fullest, has lasted to the present in spite of the relatively better position Jamaica finds itself in economically at this time. However, the companies still to a large extent, control information about market prices, reserves, alternative strategies relating to expansion of their production capacities, and most importantly technology. It can be argued, therefore, that resorting to the exploitation of its mineral resources as a strategy aimed at economic diversification, proved to have been no easy task for Jamaica. The mining companies succeeded in securing for themselves unimpeded access to Jamaica's bauxite very much on terms dictated by them. In general, these terms helped to maximize the "control" relationship as Girvan argues, "between the parent companies and the Caribbean subsidiaries and minimize and stabilize the 'regulation and revenue' relationship between the subsidiaries and the Caribbean states" (Girvan, 1976, p. 111).

West Indian political economist William Demas, in addressing the same situation from a different frame of reference, was to note at a later date that events led to continued corporate control and domination of the "commanding heights" of the economy of the English speaking West Indies. It could be clearly observed that by the end of the 1960s, giant multinational corporations had taken the place of "small merchants", influencing in every respect the economies of the countries in the region, as well as the decision-making process regarding the allocation of resources and investments. Demas noted further, that by 1968 the sugar industry, tourism, banking and insurance, manufacturing, mining of petroleum and bauxite were all dominated by multinational corporations. Although the penetration of the multinationals resulted in some growth in some key sectors, unfortunately "an independent self-sustaining process of economic development was not achieved (Demas, 1976, pp. 4-5).

With specific regard to bauxite, the multinationals had such total control that by the time Jamaica became a politically independent nation its government was forced to accept having the nation's bauxite exploited on the multinational's terms, or not having it exploited at all. Jamaica fared no better in other areas of industrial development. Indeed, as previously noted, the areas of tourism, insurance and banking, and the export of sugar and bananas were no less completely controlled. Jamaica encountered enormous handicaps resulting from colonialism. Despite major efforts to establish a viable economic base, it became increasingly evident that "an independent self-sustaining process of economic development was not achieved" (Demas, 1976, p. 5). Jamaica, very much like other Caribbean nations, continues to struggle and its problems multiply.

Succeeding political directorates, especially those which emerged after self-government in the 1950s and in the early years of political independence, adopted a philosophy of industrial development patterned on the "Puerto Rico Model" which evolved during the 1950s from the experience of Puerto Rico (Manley, 1975). With emphasis placed on the Puerto Rico Model, no serious attempt was ever undertaken to restructure agriculture or to bring the underdeveloped and backward rural areas into an overall national economic plan. Industrialization having become the key developmental strategy, emphasis was placed on inducing foreign companies through tax incentives and political stability to locate manufacturing plants, hotels, and other service industries in Jamaica. Coupled with this was a policy geared to the rapid increase in the extraction of the island's bauxite reserves.

As demonstrated in this chapter, the policies implemented by the colonial administration in Jamaica and continuing under self government in the 1950s enhanced the domination and control of the key sectors of the Jamaican economy by foreign interests. By the year 1962 when the island finally attained political independence from Britain, the giant multinational corporations of the post World War II era had as Demas noted "replaced the small merchant firms of the 18th century," (Demas, 1976, p. 5). They controlled not only sugar, the earlier primary commodity, but the mining of mineral resources, and every other area of economic, industrial and developmental importance to the island.

Although it faced the seemingly insurmountable obstacles, of foreign control of economic development, resource allocation, and economic decision-making, Jamaica decided in 1962 to become an independent nation and a member of the Commonwealth (formally the British Commonwealth). But, in making the transition from colonialism to independent national status, the Jamaican people and their government were determined to chart their own course—a course based on their concept of development, Jamaica willingly embraced independence despite a legacy of hardships inherited from a less than concerned colonial administration and the obvious economic and political uncertainties which the new nation would inevitably face. The Jamaican revolution was both peaceful and democratic. The manifestation of this democratic revolution is to be found in the desire of the Jamaican people to create an egalitarian society, one in which the fruits of their collective labor would be equitably distributed.

Notes

1. For an insightful analysis of the impact of these basic characteristics on economic planning in Jamaica, see Michael Manley's *The Politics of Change: A Jamaican Testament* (The Restructuring of a Past -Colonial Economy, p. 85.)

2. For an analysis of the impact of the population explosion on the Jamaican economy see Owen Jefferson, *The Post-War Economic Development of Jamaica*, Unwin Brothers Limited, Surry, England, 1972.

3. For an analysis of the fundamental characteristics of small economies and the problems they encounter in the developmental process see William Demas, *The Economics of Development in Small Countries with Special Reference to the Caribbean*, McGill University Press, 1965.

4. W. A. Lewis, "An Economic Play for Jamaica", *Agenda*, Vol. 3, No. 4, November 1944, p. 161.

5. Wendell Bell, *Jamaican Leaders: Political Attitudes in a New Nation*, Berkeley and Los Angeles: University of California Press, 1964, pp. 156-157.

3
Independence and the Changing of the Guard: 1962-1980

By the end of World War II, Britain began to realize that its war ravaged economy would not allow it to continue to maintain its empire and to function as a major world power. In the opinion of many analysts, acceptance of this reality came dangerously late to the British. They reluctantly accepted the fact that their policy commitments and projections far outweighed their power resources. The realities of a lessening status in world politics and the cost of imperial power prompted the Atlee Government to begin the process of divesting itself of its vast colonial empire. The process had actually begun in 1931 with passage of the Statute of Westminster under which Canada, Australia, New Zealand and the Union of South Africa became self-governing dominions. India and Pakistan became independent in 1947. Because of their positive response to British political tutelage the British West Indies were selected for early release, provided the conditions set by London were accepted by the colonies in that area.

Jamaica attained a measure of internal self government in 1957. Home rule, as it was called by the British, was a period when Jamaica sought to become virtually independent from Britain, while at the same time maintaining continued trade and other economic relations which would be in the form of developmental grants and aid to which the colonial countries saw themselves entitled. The British government, however, while desperately anxious to divest itself of what it perceived to be an economic burden, was not prepared to totally withdraw from the West Indies. Indeed, the Monroe Doctrine notwithstanding, the Caribbean area was considered of significant geostrategic importance to Britain. This consideration stemmed primarily from Britain's reluctance to accept the end of its hegemonic position in international politics.

The British government, therefore, was reluctant to dissolve its two hundred year old ties with the West Indies without installing in its colonies some form of de facto political control and establishing a system capable of maintaining their "economic viability". The political and economic structure which eventually emerged in 1958 was the British designed West Indies Federation. However, even before this structure assumed its final shape, widespread opposition to the idea of a federation was evident throughout the Caribbean. Although the need for closer association between the English-speaking Caribbean Islands dates back to the 1600s and was recognized in many earlier proposals by the Colonial Office, West Indians were always suspicious of any moves that did not originate from their own indigenous desires. Geographical size and assumed importance to England fostered by a British policy of playing one colony off against the other, helped to engender a sense of rivalry in the West Indies. Therefore, the West Indies Federation was doomed to failure even before it became a reality.[1]

The West Indies Federation

In view of the foregoing, it is appropriate at this point to undertake a brief analysis of the West Indies Federation and Jamaica's role in its demise. The intention is to bring into focus some of the principal reasons why Jamaica and the other participating countries sought independence and resisted the concept of a federation. By 1945 several political figures who advocated independence for Britain's Caribbean colonies had emerged as undisputed leaders in their respective countries. In Jamaica, William Alexander Bustamente led the Jamaica Labor Party (JLP) and its workers union arm, the Bustamente Industrial Trade Union. Actively pursuing the role of opposition leader was Norman Washington Manley of the Peoples National Party (PNP). In Trinidad, the legendary Uriah "Buzz" Butler led a large following of oil field workers and other laborers. Barbados saw the emergence of Grantly Adams as a labor leader. Adams, like Manley of Jamaica, was an Oxford trained lawyer.[2]

Due to the efforts of these indigenous leaders, as well as other native political and social activists, there developed by 1945 profound changes in the minds of most West Indians. Political and social activists such as Marcus Garvey had earlier encouraged the formation of political parties aimed at securing a larger share of representation in the colonial legislature. "Political sentiment", as Knight argued, "found expression through individual radicals such as Sandy Cox and J. A. G. Smith." Jamaicans who returned after service in war theaters in Europe, North Africa and the Mediterranean agitated for change. Their agitation helped to increase a sense of self-consciousness among

Jamaicans which manifested itself in various forms of political and social protests demanding immediate changes in the relationship between the colonial administration and Jamaicans (Knight, 1978, p. 178). It was by then quite evident that the fires of social and political change were burning brightly. The foundations for such changes were already long in place. Leaders such as Robert Osbern in 1860, and before him, Jamaicans George William Gordeon and Paul Bogle, Andrew Cipiriani in Trinidad, as well as many others, had foretold by their respective political actions the demise of West Indian colonialism. In Jamaica Gordeon and Bogle fought the oligarchy created by the old representative system where the white sugar estate owners virtually controlled the colonial government. Paule Bogel played a leading role in the Morant Bay rebellion of 1865 for which he was hanged. Nevertheless, his efforts and the uprising set the stage for constitutional changes, that greatly curtailed the power of the planter/merchant class which ruled Jamaica since 1660. These political changes undoubtedly created the environment that eventually forced the British to relinquish their hold on the colonies (Sherlock, 1966, p. 53). These leaders did not advocate a federation of any kind, they spoke of independence with regard to individual sovereign status.

The British, however, had other ideas. Thus, in 1945, the colonial governors of the West Indian colonies were instructed by the Secretary of State for the Colonies to introduce the question of federation before the respective colonial legislatures for debate. Opposition to a British inspired federation was almost immediate. This initial step was followed in 1947 by a conference of West Indian leaders. Prominent West Indian leaders at the time, specifically Grantly Adams in Barbadoes, Eric Williams in Trinidad, Manley and Bustamante in Jamaica and Jagan in Guyana, acceeded to the idea of a federation and agreed to attend the Montego Bay conference because they assumed that independence would not be given to each island seperately, but would be conceded only to a federation. In facing reality the leaders saw federation as a necessary prelude to independence. According to Mordecai, the leaders "wanted federation in order to realize their nationalistic aspirations." They were therefore willing to play the British at their game (Mordecai, 1968, pp. 32-33). The conference was held in Montego Bay, where Jamaica accepted in principle the basic outlines of a federation wherein each constituent unit would retain complete control over all matters excepting those specifically assigned to the Federal Government (Hewan, 1971, p. 49).

A closer examination of the discussions held in the Montego Bay meeting reveals that the proposed federation had no clear focus. There was an almost complete absence of any agreement concerning the scope and aims of a federated West Indies. The Montego Bay conference was preceded by a meeting of the Caribbean Labour Congress in Kingston a couple of days earlier. That gathering focused on federation and unanimously passed a memorandum and a "comprehensively outlined draft federal constitution for presentation at Montego Bay." The memorandum called for "a federation that would provide responsible government equivalent to Dominion Status". It also demanded that each unit of the federation be accorded constitutional advances which would bring it to internal self-government. Significantly, in the statement that introduced the draft bill, the Congress warned it would reject "any form of limited or partial approach to this fundamental goal" (Mordecai, 1986, p. 35).

It is important to note that Manley, Adams, and Gomes of Trinidad had agreed in advance to press the resolution, which others had also pledged to support. Bustamante, whose presence was critical, absented himself. The alternatives examined involved either pressing for postponement of federation until all the units atained a similar constitutional level or to embark immediately on a federation with dominion status. The resolution from the Labour Congress failed to seize center stage at the Montego Bay conference. Three vital factors contributed to this state of affairs: (a) Bustamante's negative characterization of federation as a "federation of paupers" pushed by the British to escape their responsibilities; (b) the subtle opposition of the conference chairman, Secretary of State Arthur Creech-Jones, to the Caribbean Labour Congress resolution who felt it was "outside the immediate terms of reference of this Conference"; and (c) the discovery by the political leaders at the conference that they were not the only spokesmen for what the West Indies wanted.

Most important were so-called non-political "neutrals", primarily business and professional men eminent in public life on both sides of the Caribbean, who "not only spoke up with authority," as Mordecai noted, "but undertook the lion's share of Committee work" (Mordecai, 1986, pp. 35-36). The conservative counsel of these men influenced to a great extent the direction of the Conference.

Each participant's proposal embodied a different conception of what colony should or should not be incorporated into the venture. In reality, most if not all were suspicious of Jamaica because of the belief that that island sought to dominate the others. The inability of the conference participants to arrive at an agreement can be attributed to the fact that a West Indian federation as devised by the British was not in keeping with what West Indian leaders had in mind for the region. This was the case even though some West Indians, mostly third and fourth generation children of the planter/merchant class, had at various times in the past proposed the idea of a federation. These ideas were built upon the concept of equals dealing with equals as politically and economically free peoples. In contrast, British idea was predicated upon the maintenance of the Empire as a closed and viable entity ruled from London. Gordon K. Lewis pointed out that "Official British opinion, throughout viewed federation not as a vehicle for West Indian self-government, but overwhelmingly, as a problem of colonial administrative convenience" (Lewis, 1968, p. 344).

An examination of the voluminous documentation supporting Lewis' opinion, in Westminster debates, royal commission reports, Colonial Office memoranda, as well as the published correspondence between the Colonial Secretary and individual colonial governors substantiates the argument put forth by the leading analysts of the period, such as John Mordecai, William G. Demas, Wendell Bell, and C. L. R. James, that the most persistently recurring reason evoked in support of federation was the greater economy and improved administrative efficiency federation would ensure. Notwithstanding the numerous problems still unresolved, especially on the question of self government, the West Indies Federation became a reality in 1958. The federation, however, was short lived. Very few people, especially West Indian leaders and their publics, had any illusions as to the eventual fate of the federation. Consquently, very few were surprised at its demise.

The level of insularity existing in the Caribbean is such that some people familiar with the region have on a number of occasions entertained doubts whether a federation of the countries in the area could in fact remain a viable entity. It was therefore not surprising when a number of major and minor irritants, namely taxation, intra-regional trade, and the role and function of the Federal Prime Minister, began to adversely affect relations between the unit governments. In time these problems led to a conflict between the Premier of Trinidad and Tobago, Dr. Eric Williams, and the Federal Prime Minister, Sir. Grantly Adams, over the Chaguaramas United States Air Force Base in Trinidad. The base was established under the World War II Lend Lease Agreement between the U. S. and Britain. Trinidad wanted the U. S. to vacate the base and felt that the Federal Government was conspiring with Britain and the U. S. to frustrate its aspirations.

A second conflict of equal importance emerged between Jamaica and Trinidad when Jamaica proposed the construction of a oil refinery in Jamaica. Trinidad's opposition to this proposal on the grounds that it would adversely affect its oil industry elicited strong objections from Jamaica. These and many other problems including a charge that the Federal Prime Minister was antagonistic toward the larger states of the federation, (and had publicly questioned the intelligence of Jamaicans and Trinidadians) culminated in a sequence of announcements by Jamaica, Trinidad and Tobago, Barbados, and Guyana of their intentions to withdraw from the Federation. Following Jamaica's and Trinidad's decision to withdraw, the remaining eight countries explored the possibility of continuing the federation. This, however, failed because of a lack of an economic base which only Jamaica and Trinidad could offer at the time.[3]

Accepting the inevitability of the federation's demise, many indigenous West Indian leaders sought instead to secure a firm political footing in their respective countries. What emerged was a united front whose sole aim was to secure individual independence for each country in the federation. The Jamaican political leader Alexander Bustamente, who had consistently voiced a distaste for any form of federation, led Jamaica's campaign for withdrawal from the organization. His efforts forced Premier Norman Manley to call a national referendum to decide whether Jamaicans wished to remin in the federation. The proposed Jamaican referendum, an event upon which the future of federation hinged, prompted similar proposals throughout the West Indies. Premier Eric Williams of Trinidad left no doubt that his country had in place alternative policies in the event Jamaica seceded from the federation.

Norman Manley, who advocated federation as the path that would lead to independence for the Caribbean countries, called a national referendum in Jamaica because he believed (mistakenly) that most Jamaicans shared his commitment to a West Indian Federation. Manley and the rest of the West Indies were to discover on September 19, 1961, the day of the referendum, that Jamaicans were overwhelmingly opposed to a federation with the other territories. Of the 61% of the total electorate that went to the polls, 54.1% gave a decisive "yes" to Bustamente's rallying slogan "Independence—yes, Federation—no". The voting was strictly along party lines. In the minds of some observers the voters in the referendum understood very little about the issues involved. For Jamaica, the result of the referendum meant that island would seek political independence as a nation.[4]

The Road To Independence

The failure of the West Indies Federation was the event that rekindled a new wave of sentiment for nationhood in the region. Indeed, the historical tradition of insularity in the Caribbean has been attributed as the primary cause of the federation's collapse. The roots of the actual causes, however, are much more complex. They are the result of the Caribbean tradition of separatism and of colonial fragmentation fostered to a great extent by British political doctrine which included the age old concept of 'divide and conquer'. Some observers attribute other causes to the failure to meet the three conditions that Sir Hubert Elvin Ronce defined in December 1952:

The prerequisites for federation are many but the outstanding points are three. (1) A general and sufficiently strong desire for a federal grouping; (2) An equal desire to retain for the units some at any rate of the powers of government; (3) A capacity to work a federal system.[5]

It is important to note that none of these prerequisites were ever seriously ingrained in West Indian political thought or practice by the British colonialists during the era of political tutelage (Hewan, P. 55, 1971).

Jamaica prepared for political independence after the results of the 1961 referendum. Following a number of preparatory conferences held in London as well as in Jamaica, an order for a new constitution was adopted and came into effect on July 25, 1962, thereby establishing the legal framework for the transfer of sovereign authority from London to Kingston.

By virtue of the Jamaica Independence Act, Jamaica formally assumed independent status on August 6, 1962 as a Dominion partner within the Commonwealth of Nations. This ended one of the longest, unbroken periods of colonial rule in modern history, three hundred and seven years. The September 19, 1961 referendum chose the political party and leader that would form the first government of an independent Jamaica. Prior to the granting of independence there were two major political parties in Jamaica, the Jamaica Labor Party (JLP) and the People's National Party (PNP). Having rejected the PNP and its leader, Norman Washington Manley, who was committed to the federation as a path to independence, Jamaicans selected William Alexander Bustamente and the JLP as the leader and political party they wanted to form the first government of an independent Jamaica.

Much has been written regarding the events leading to Jamaica becoming an independent nation. Analysts have contended that events which were unfolding in the West Indies at the time played into the hands of Alexander Bustamente. Bustamente and the JLP in a "rump" convention in November

1960, had demonstrated their commitment to the independence route by affirming "their faith in the future of this country and its people to stand on its own, and to pursue its own course to nationhood and prosperity without the complications and conflicts of outside interests."[6] Mordecai contends that the position of Bustamente and his party on the issue of independence for Jamaica introduced in very simple terms a "national motif" (Mordecia, 1968, p. 398) that elicited an emotional response from the Jamaican people that spared them the task of trying to fully comprehend the confusing details of a regional alliance in which they did not wish to participate. A 'no' vote on the question of federation became identified with the vision of a complete and real Jamaican nationhood (Mordeci, P. 397-98, 1968).

Contrary to the belief commonly expressed at the time, that the true meaning of independence would not be fully understood, the building of a nation in Jamaica was a cogently unifying undertaking. The nation building experience involved strata of the society that had been as critical to the country's stability and future prospects as similar groups had been in Europe and the United States of America. Indeed, as Anthony Payne contends, Jamaicans notwithstanding some aspects of color and racial divisions within their society—a legacy left by the British—are painfully cognizant of the fact that they share a common history in being originally immigrants to the land they now call home (Payne, 1988, p. 7). Thus, it can be argued that the fundamental principles underlying independence are fully understood by Jamaicans and have helped to foster the process of unity, instilling a remarkable and confident sense of national identity.

The Political System

Jamaica's emergence into the modern political world has not been entirely tranquil. Indeed, the growing pains associated with new nation status manifested themselves in various ways, impacting significantly on the conduct of the nation's domestic as well as international affairs. Independence, while no doubt a most welcome change from the status quo, nevertheless forced Jamaican society at all levels to undertake an ongoing process of self-examination. Jamaicans rediscovered the importance of their history, they saw in the process the strength of character and fortitude of spirit inherited from such giants as Sam Sharp, General Cudjoe, Nanny, Tacky, Paul Bogel, and George William Gordon. Guiding that exercise was the widespread belief that whatever efforts were needed to solve the nation's numerous problems they had to be indigenously Jamaican. The politically painful but economically comforting yoke of colonialism would not be available as a "safety net."

The knowledge that the future of the nation was fully in the hands of the Jamaican people helped to forge a national political identity which in turn created a democratic environment. A unique feature of this environment is clearly evident in the nation's constitution. Jamaica is the first nation to have written in its new constitution (1962), a provision guaranteeing a "leader of the opposition" although making no reference to political parties. This provision ensures at a minimum a two party political system and makes it virtually impossible for a one party state to be created. When viewed within the context of contemporary Third World politics, which is characterized increasingly by one party states, the dynamic aspects of the foregoing provision is of particular significance. Moreover, since independence, Jamaica has experienced seven very competitive general elections, none of which were blatantly rigged as has been the experience of Guyana, Nigeria and many other Third World Countries.

Before becoming an independent nation, Jamaica had in place a strong multi-party tradition. This experience has served the Island very well. The 1938 disturbances referred to earlier signalled the beginning of a new and interesting period in the modern political history of the nation. While the outburst of discontent did not initially center upon political demands, it served as a catalyst for the creation of trade unions and political parties (Hurwitz, 1971, p. 194). The first political party, the People's Political Party (PPP), was formed by Marcus Garvey in 1929 and experienced a short life span. However, as a result of the 1938 disturbances, the People's National Party (PNP) was created by Norman Washington Manley. This was Jamaica's first true mass party.

Other mass political parties followed on the heels of the PNP, such as the Jamaica Labor Party (JLP) founded in 1942 by William Alexander Bustamente and the Jamaica Democratic Party (JDP) formed in 1944 by a group of middle class Jamaican businessmen. The JDP like the PPP before it had a very short existence. Presently at least three political parties actively participate in the electoral process. The third party, the Worker's Party of Jamaica (WPJ) headed by Oxford-educated Professor Trevor Monroe of the University of the West Indies, although having only limited electoral success, is very much a part of the political environment.

The two major political parties in Jamaica are the People's National Party and the Jamaica Labor Party. These two parties have challenged each other for control of the political arena for more than 42 years. While some of these contests have been acrimonious, the freedom to participate in the political process and the absolute right to support the political party of one's choice and to vote one's conscience have been upheld and fully supported at all levels of society. Indeed, freedom of thought, expression, worship and assembly are well entrenched principles in Jamaican political culture.

Jamaica's government is a modified form of parliamentary democracy consisting of an Executive, a Legislature and a Judiciary. The Executive is a cabinet of at least 12 Ministers headed by a Prime Minister, all whom must be a member of the House of Representatives. The legislature is a bicameral parliament, the House of Representatives being elected by universal adult suffrage on a constituency basis. The second chamber, the Senate, is appointed by the Governor-General on the advice of the Prime Minister and the Leader of the opposition. Both chambers are represented in the Cabinet. The Judiciary is comprised of a Court of Appeal, a Supreme Court and other lesser courts. Jamaica's legal system is based on British Common Law and Practice. The fundamental rights and freedoms of the individual are entrenched in the Constitution. Upon achieving independence Jamaica opted for membership in the British Commonwealth (now called the Commonwealth of Nations) with Queen Elizabeth II as head of state represented by a local Governor-General.

The political and economic events of Jamaica's 27 years of independence are firmly rooted in the two major political parties. The structures of the parties are embedded in their trade union organizations which have remained viable and secure throughout the years. Several issues during the early years of independence created significant party differences. This was evident in the tensions caused by the maldistribution of wealth and income among the constituent elements of the nation. Hurwitz argues that the PNP was fundamentally different from the JLP in its call for "common ownership" of large agricultural industries as well as the nationalization of utilities. As early as 1965 the PNP called for the nationalization of the Jamaica Public Service Company, the country's gas and electric utility, which at the time was completely foreign owned. The PNP also argued that enterprises such as the telephone service, the cement factory and other essential services "should not be regarded as legitimate sources of private profit" (Hurwitz, 1971, pp. 218-19).

While there are substantial differences between the two major parties, they are not far apart on the question of programs relating to economic development. They both have a strong commitment to land reform. The two parties also favor a policy of economic development which emphasizes ownership by Jamaicans and the employment of Jamaicans in agricultural, financial, and industrial businesses irrespective of the size and ownership of the enterprise. Although the parties do have different emphases in their respective economic development programs, in that the JLP persued a path of dependent development while the PNP sought a more self-reliant independent route, there have been very few political conflicts resulting from these differences. The major differences observed between the two parties are in the area of civil liberties. Here the parties are much further apart and the difference are more fractious than those in most other areas. In the case of the PNP, its program calls for the creation of an ombudsman in Jamaica who would deal with the numerous problems encountered in the Administrative Level between government and Civil Servants primarily over wage and personnel matters. The JLP for its part, argues that workers and unions in some cases have become uncontrollable. There is also the ongoing problem of the power Government Ministers can exercise over professionals in their ministries. These and other problems point to the role an independent ombudsman could play in helping to alleviate internal strife. The JLP opposes the creation of an ombudsman and refuses to entertain any such proposal.

Political patronage is a widely accepted and important aspect of Jamaica's political system. Both political parties attempt to attract and keep supporters by providing for their welfare through the award of jobs. In a country with the high unemployment rate that Jamaica normally has, the party that controls the government acquires extensive power through the allocation of government jobs. A consequence of this has been that both parties have imposed a high degree of victimization on each other's supporters while accusing the other party of exclusive use of the practice. Jamaican political behavior since independence provides ample support for Hurwitz's contention that "the ethics of party patronage, as opposed to non-partisan appointments, is the orientation of Jamaica's political culture" (Hurwitz, 1971, p. 221).

Until the early 1970s, political patronage with a civil liberties orientation formed the basis for political party conflict in Jamaica. Up to that time differences in ideology were minimal if not nonexistent. Indeed, it can be argued that during the twenty five years between 1944 and 1969 politics in Jamaica was controlled exclusively by two political parties both enjoying the unswerving support of roughly 40% respectively of the electorate, with the remaining 20% acting as a swing vote ready to call into question any excesses or failure to fulfill campaign promises by the party in control of government. That the parties were constantly aware of this fact rebuts John D. Forbes's contention that the political parties "did not offer the Jamaican electorate any dynamic choice of social and economic policy" (Forbes, 1985, p. 11). The fact is that they did offer alternative choices. Indeed the PNP from its inception offered the choice of a socialist path to political and economic development, stressing the need for self-reliance and local control over the means of production. The JLP sought to avoid ideological labeling by following a more conservative path stressing a dependent mode of economic development in which foreign investment would play a dominant role. The parties were however, restricted to the limited socio-economic parameters within which they were able to operate. It is important to remember that Jamaican political parties began their careers within a colonialist environment hampered by the social stratification that prevailed as well as the economic constraints placed on their activities. One can argue that very little has changed in the politics of today, the restrictions though somewhat different in respect to control still have their roots in the old system.

The restricted socio-economic parameters acted as a natural barrier to achieving the levels of social, political, and economic development necessary to prevent the type of social upheaval always possible in developing Third World countries. Traditionally, the wealthy elite controls the essential areas of society such as education, health facilities, food distribution, and the distribution of economic resources. In the case of Jamaica the inequality in these essentials was further aggravated by the lack of real political power in the hands of the masses. In fact, the problem was soon to manifest itself in the social and political disturbances of 1968. Known as the Rodney Riots,[7] that episode must be viewed as a turning point in the post-independence history of Jamaica. The disturbances began as a result of the government banning from Jamaica, Dr. Walter Rodney a well liked and respected lecturer at the University of the West Indies (UWI). The government's action led to a protest march in the city of Kingston by students at the University. The protest march was broken up by police which led to further violence and mass looting by the unemployed and urban poor. The crisis lasted for at least two days resulting in loss of life and millions of dollars in destroyed property. This event was, as Payne has argued, "a telling commentary on the state of affairs" in Jamaica, coinciding as it were with the Black Liberation movement in the United States of America (Payne, 1988, p. 14).

The disturbance highlighted the failure of the Jamaican political system to adequately address the pressing issues of unemployment, underemployment and the maldistribution of wealth. Of equal importance, it attracted the interest of the United States in view of the allegedly "socialist" leadership of the disturbances. The violence directed against property, which resulted spontaneously from the depressed economic conditions rather than any ideological awakening, far surpassed anything witnessed in Jamaica since the 1938 disturbances. Until 1968 the Jamaican political system had succeeded in containing the explosive implications of the socio-economic structure, gaining for Jamaica a world wide reputation for political stability. Stone points to the fact that party, rather than class or race, was developed as the focus and collective frame of reference for the politically conscious in the nation (Stone, 1973, p. 51).

The Jamaican political system, shaken to its core by the 1968 events, underwent a metamorphosis in its ideological orientation. It became apparent to the political elite that the mode of economic development of the country had generated the discontent and that the political system had failed to contain it. Evidence further suggests that the 1968 upheavals were, as Payne argued, more or less a vivid "example of demonstrative rather than revolutionary violence." As such they must be seen as "emotionally charged rather than coolly planned, short lived rather than the prelude to continuing disorder". They are more accurately described as "a kind of cathartic outburst by the dispossessed" (Payne, 1988, p. 31). Indeed the disturbances were a forewarning to the political and economic structures of what was in store for the future if immediate steps were not taken to correct the social inadequacies of the Jamaican political economy and thus draw the dispossessed back into the mainstream of national political life.

While the JLP as the governing party was forced to respond to the Rodney riots by emphasizing coercion, the PNP after tacitly siding with the government, took a new direction suggested by its founder Norman Manley who was then nearing the end of his political career. Manley told the PNP that the task of his generation was the achieving of political independence for Jamaica. However, the torch of leadership had to be passed to a new generation who would be charged with responsibility for ensuring the social and economic well being of the Jamaican people. The mantle of leadership for the assumption of this responsibility passed to Norman Manley's son Michael who became the leader of the PNP in 1969. Coupled with the upheavals of 1968, Michael Manley's ascension to the leadership of the PNP marked the turning point of political party activity in Jamaica. Whether accurately or not, the PNP was perceived as the party articulating the legitimate aspirations of the poor masses, voicing their discontent arising from the joblessness, victimization, coercion and corruption associated with the JLP government (Payne, 1988, p. 32).

Events Leading to the 1980 Election:
Changing of the Guard

The People's National Party (PNP) won the 1972 General Election following a leadership and policy change in 1969. By the time of the 1972 election the feeling among a sizable portion of the population was that the Jamaica Labor Party, which had been in charge of the government since 1962, had failed to lead the island away from a situation in which national wealth continued to be controlled exclusively by a few elite families and by foreign interests (Payne, 1988, p. 30). It was felt that the Jamaican masses were systematically excluded from sharing in the wealth of the nation. Coupled with this was the belief that although foreign investors had provided some new job opportunities, they were nevertheless exporting vast amounts of profits to their parent companies rather than reinvesting these profits in Jamaica (Forbes, 1985, pp. 13-16).

While some of these charges had merit, the fact could not be denied that the JLP had contributed immensely to the building of a free and independent nation within the constraints of the social, political and economic structures inherited from the colonial era. By the end of its first government in 1967 Jamaica had developed a unique national outlook that has instilled a sense of confidence and nationalistic pride in the individual's identity as a Jamaican. The culture of the lower class, long considered inferior, had been given new status and recognition by the government. Accordingly as, Hurwitz and Hurwitz point out, Jamaican leaders have been quick to give status to the nationalism and the nationalist movement which legitimized their power (Hurwitz and Hurwitz, 1971, pp. 216-17).

British honors long coveted by leaders throughout the Commonwealth Caribbean were abolished in 1968 to be replaced by National or Jamaican honors. Jamaica, led by the JLP, was the only former colony to abolish knighthood replacing it with the Order of Jamaica. The new rank of national hero was exalted and placed above other honors. This honor was awarded posthumously to Marcus Garvey, Paul Bogle, and George William Gordon, Jamaica's first national heroes. This honor was also awarded to Alexander Bustamente and Norman Washington Manley in 1969 thus recognizing the two Jamaicans most responsible for the social, political and economic progress in modern times. The new nationalism fostered by the JLP in the early post-independence years effectively replaced the western cultural tradition as the primary standard of value. In its place has been created a unique Jamaican culture (Hurwitz and Hurwitz, P. 218, 1971).

Prior to the 1972 election several very important issues were to emerge which created differences and subsequent tensions between the two major parties. First of these was the problem regarding the distribution of wealth and income among the various strata of society. Proposals suggested by the PNP advocated a policy of "common ownership" of major agricultural enterprises as well as the outright nationalization of public utility industries. These would include the Jamaica Public Service Company (electricity), and the Jamaica Telephone Company. Indeed that was the theme featured in the PNP's 1967 "Plan for Progress" election campaign. As noted by the Hurwitzes, nationalization of all public utilities, cement production, and transportation was demanded in the name of "government of and for the people" (Hurwitz and Hurwitz, 1971, p. 219).

There are many supporters as well as detractors of the PNP who have argued that the party first showed its socialist leanings in 1974. Anthony Payne in his analysis of this period wrote that in 1974 the PNP government "startled the Jamaican people" when it announced that it had converted to socialism and proclaimed that Jamaica would henceforth be considered a socialist country (Payne, 1988, p. 34). Although there is some validity to Payne's contention, The Hurwitzes noted that in 1970 Michael Manley, upon succeeding his father as leader of the PNP in 1969, had magnified the concept of public ownership to embrace "a share for Jamaicans in the ownership of the bauxite companies" (Hurwitz and Hurwitz, 1971, p. 219-20).

Thus, it can be argued that even before the PNP took over the reins of government in 1972 its ideological reorientation and policy perspectives were patently clear. There is evidence to support the contention that an ideological orientation was already discernable even as early as 1969 in Norman Manley's farewell speech to the party. Possibly realizing that his call for public ownership of the bauxite industry would antagonize the United States government, Michael Manley in an apparent attempt to clarify his position on the bauxite question noted in a parliamentary debate on the budget that every phase of the aluminum industry operating in Jamaica "should be owned by government, workers, and private shareholders together". This statement was interpreted as implying that the PNP intended to adopt a new concept of joint ownership including the private and public sectors of the economy (Hurwitz and Hurwitz, 1971, p. 220).

Another area of fundamental difference between PNP and JLP modes of economic policy involved taxation. Leading members of the PNP argued for many years that the nation's income tax laws were weighted heavily in favor of areas that did not serve the national interest. Manley also called for additional taxes to be levied against the bauxite industry. In other areas of economic development, however, the parties have not been as far apart. Both have been and are seriously committed to land reform. Both parties favor a policy of economic development that places emphasis on ownership by Jamaicans and the employment of Jamaicans in financial, agricultural and industrial enterprises regardless of the amount of their capital investments.

Despite the differences that existed between the two parties, there was very little overt political partisan violence. This is somewhat surprising since even before independence was achieved, Jamaicans demonstrated an enthusiasm for political parties and campaigns not equaled in other areas of the Caribbean. They also, in isolated cases, resorted to violence as in the "Rodney" and subsequent West Kingston disturbances. However, the incidents were in the nature of spontaneous outbursts against social conditions rather than sustained uses of violence against the government or a specific political party. Since independence party politics in Jamaica has been largely free of violence.

By the late 1960s and early 1970s a dramatic change came over the Jamaican political scene. Both major parties had lost their original leaders. First the JLP saw the emergence of Donald Sangster, formerly a deputy leader, as leader of the party in 1967 following the resignation of Alexander Bustamante. Sangster's reign lasted only two months as he died in office shortly after the JLP's victory in the 1967 general election. The person who succeeded Sangster was Hugh Lawson Shearer, a distant cousin of both Bustamante and Manley. Shearer came to the leadership post after extensive trade union activity, as well as having served in the Kingston and Saint Andrew Parish Council in 1947 and the Senate in 1962. He also held the posts of government spokesman and adviser for foreign affairs and chief of Jamaica's delegation to the United Nations (Hurwitz and Hurwitz, 1971, pp. 224-25).

The JLP government in power from independence until 1972, elected to continue the policies of the pre-independence era. Thus, the economic growth of the late 1950s continued into the 1960s. Manufacturing, which by 1965 had shown enormous growth, was by then contributing 15 percent of GDP. The new bauxite-alumina industry comprised 10% of GDP. Tourism, a major component of economic development, experienced a phenomenal increase between 1950 and 1965, as indicated in tables 3.1 and 3.2. Despite this impressive performance in the economy as shown in tables 3.3, 3.4 and 3.5, it soon became quite apparent that the socio-political as well as the economic

TABLE 3.1 Contribution of the Tourist Industry to National Income and Retained Foreign Exchange Earnings, 1959-1969.

	Local Share of Tourist Expenditure J$million	Col.(1) as Percent of National Income	Col.(1) as Percent of Total Retained Foreign Exchange Earnings
1959	12.0	4.4	10.1
1960	17.2	4.5	12.1
1961	17.6	4.3	11.3
1962	15.8	3.6	9.7
1963	16.2	3.5	8.9
1964	18.8	3.8	9.9
1965	27.8	5.2	13.4
1966	33.6	5.9	15.4
1967	34.7	5.7	15.3
1968	43.9	6.7	17.6
1969	46.7	6.5	16.5

Source: Jefferson, 1972, p. 179.

TABLE 3.2 Growth of Visitor Accommodation, 1955-69

Year	Number of Beds	Percentage Change
1955	3,300	—
1956	3,600	+9.1
1957	4,200	+16.7
1958	4,700	+11.9
1959	5,800	+23.4
1960	6,140	+5.8
1961	6,758	+10.0

TABLE 3.2 Growth of Visitor Accommodation, 1955-69 (con't.)

Year	Number of Beds	Percentage Change
1962	7,471	+10.5
1963	7,563	+1.2
1964	7,395	-2.2
1965	7,941	+7.3
1966	8,250	+3.9
1967	8.911	+8.0
1968	9,616	+7.9
1969	10,950	+13.9

Source: Jamaica Tourist Board, Travel Statistics, 1969.

TABLE 3.3 Growth Rates of Output Within the Manufacturing Sector 1950-68

Sub-sector	Growth Rate (Per cent per annum)
Sugar, Rum and Molasses	2.7
Food and Beverages	7.9
Tobacco Products	5.5
Textile and Garments	10.7
Furniture and Fixtures	7.1
Cement and Clay Products	11.3
Chemicals and Chemical Products	5.8
Metal Products	9.6
Other Industries	8.8
Total	7.6

Source: Jefferson, 1972, p. 133. Adapted from National Income and Product Accounts.

Table 3.4 Exports of Manufactured Goods 1950-1968

Year	Exports of Manufactured Goods* J$'000	Export of Manufactured Goods as percentage of Total Domestic Exports	Exports of Manufactured Goods as percentage of Domestic Exports excluding Bauxite and Alumina
1950	1,148	3.9	3.9
1956	2,092	2.7	3.8
1957	2,260	2.3	4.0
1958	3,028	3.2	6.0
1959	3,316	3.7	6.6
1960	5,308	4.8	9.4
1961	7,042	5.8	11.5
1962	9,646	7.8	15.0
1963	10,066	7.2	12.4
1964	11,274	7.4	13.5
1965	10,878	7.3	13.7
1966	12,106	7.5	14.3
1967	13,610	8.5	16.6
1968	16,584	9.3	18.3

* Excluding sugar, other foods and beverages and petroleum products.
Source: Jefferson, 1972, p. 138.

policies of the JLP were proving to be inadequate in meeting the needs of the Jamaican people, particularly the poor masses (Jefferson, 1971, pp. 132-36).

The period of JLP rule lasting from 1962 to 1972 can be regarded as one of ever increasing prosperity for the upper and expanding middle classes, with most of the economic growth during this period stimulated by large foreign investments coming mainly from Canada and the United States. However, the jobs created by these new sources of investment proved insufficient to cope with the increases in the island's labor force, whose growth was estimated at about

TABLE 3.5 Contribution of Main Sectors to Gross Domestic Product

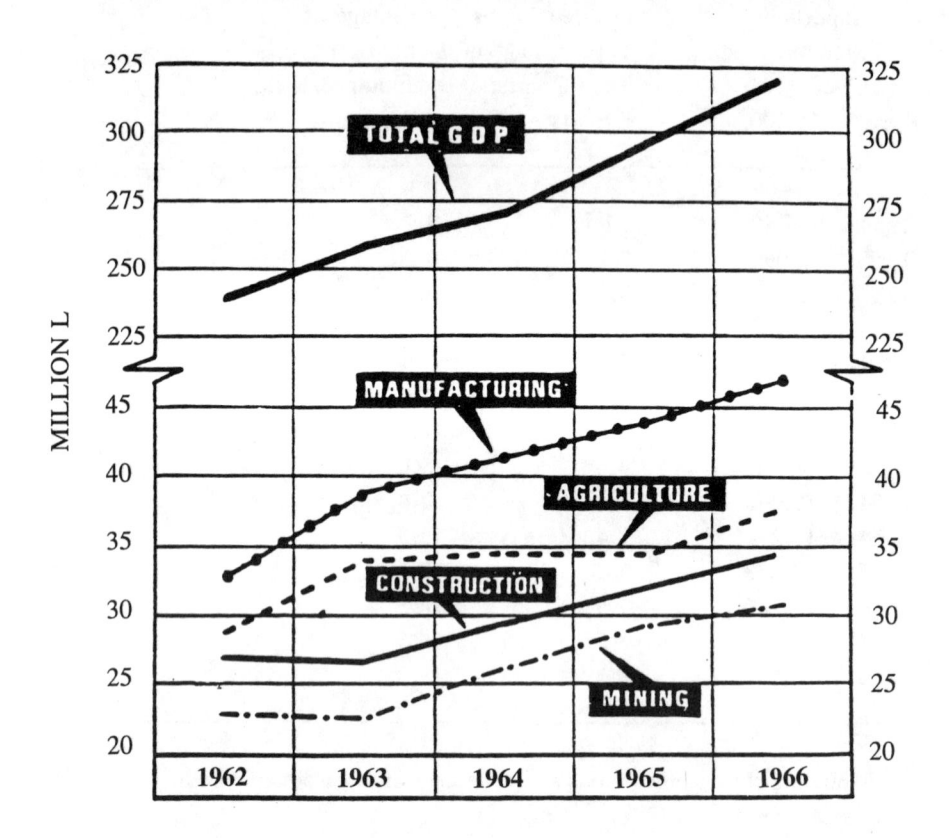

Source: National Planning Agency, Jamaica.

23,000 annually. Adding to the problem was the alarming rate of growth of public sector spending for which the newly independent government had to borrow as well as increase taxes in order to provide the necessary services to the population (Forbes, 1985, p. 14).

The JLP government under Hugh Shearer sustained economic growth. However, by 1970 his administration had gained a reputation for factionalism, weak management, and damaging corruption. This seriously weakened the JLP's chances for victory in the 1972 elections as the party fortunes continued to slide with increasing speed into a political tailspin (Stephens and Stephens, 1986, pp. 56-58). It was evident by the time the election was called that the PNP led by Michael Manley was unbeatable. While Shearer and the JLP campaigned on the issue of the strong economic growth in the 1960s, Michael Manley and the PNP focussed on rising unemployment as well as on an appealing brand of populist politics that promised to create an egalitarian society where all would share equally in the island's wealth. Manley and the PNP hammered home the egalitarian theory and used the prosperity of the 1960s against the JLP by pointing out that the benefits of economic growth were not distributed widely or equally among the electorate. The results of the election were devastating for the JLP in that the country responded to the PNP's election slogan "Better Must Come" and gave the party thirty-seven of the fifty-three seats in the House of Representatives and a commanding 56% of the popular vote.

Michael Manley became Prime Minister of Jamaica for the first time in 1972. The Manley years and his policy of "Democratic Socialism" will be analyzed fully in Chapter Four, It is sufficient to state here that the period from 1972 to 1980 aroused more international interest in Jamaica than in any other country in the Commonwealth Caribbean (Payne, 1988, p. 60). During the eight and a half years of the PNP regime, Jamaica, as Michael Manley himself has stated, was witness to "some of the more controversial events" in its short but colorful history. These events were eventually to spell doom for the PNP and Michael Manley as he was never again able to develop "a coherent approach to the management of the political economy" (Payne, 1988, p. 79). Manley's fortunes failed rapidly after a striking beginning in 1972. After 1976 his pattern of governing was one of endless indecisiveness in which he flirted alternately with the Jamaican political left and international right while the nation's economy deteriorated.

In 1974 when the PNP announced its intentions to pursue a socialist path, internal conflicts within the opposition JLP resulted in the election of Edward Seaga to succeed Hugh Shearer as party leader. Seaga immediately began to play a very active role as leader of the opposition (1974-1980). A Harvard trained economist with expertise in financial, cultural and social-development Seaga brought to the leadership of the JLP a highly disciplined, hard working image. While this image did not endear Seaga to the common man it nevertheless sent a message to the electorate as well as the international community that the party intended to be taken seriously. Seaga being of a more serious disposition than Shearer, continued on a much more personal and acrimonious scale the traditional JLP-PNP leadership rivalry while earning for himself a reputation as a highly disciplined, hard-working, and intellectual leader.

Seaga led the JLP into the 1980 elections which unseated Michael Manley and the PNP. He had first engaged Manley in the 1976 elections. This election witnessed major realignments in support for both parties. It also witnessed an unprecedented level of political violence and polarization on ideological and policy issues. To many observers the 1976 political contest between Seaga and Manley was the dress rehearsal for the 1980 campaign, thus the October 30, 1980 election pitting a socialist PNP led by Manley against a democratic JLP led by Seaga proved to be the most violent, divisive and important in the island's history. The personal and ideological antagonism that existed between Seaga and Manley filtered down through their two parties and in turn caused a rising political polarization between the rival camps and within the Jamaican society as a whole (Forbes, 1985, p. 30).

Party rivalry further intensified with the introduction of opposing external elements, primarily the United States and Cuba. John D. Forbes in his analysis of the 1980 election noted that the two major political parties, as well as the Worker's Party of Jamaica (formed in the mid 1970s), had employed and armed thugs and criminals at election time (Forbes, 1985, p. 32). But Forbes, who served as political counselor in the United States Embassy in Kingston (1980-1983), failed to mention that the guns given to the "political thugs" were supplied by the United States and Cuba. Evidence, although circumstantial, led to the conclusion that the U.S. Army M16s, the favorite weapon of the PNP came to Jamaica from Vietnam via Cuba along with Russian made AK-47s, the main assault weapon of the Cuban Armed Forces. Likewise Bushmaster submachine guns along with other U.S. Army M16s used by the JLP entered Jamaica from Miami. Both the PNP government and the JLP opposition at the time entertained strong suspicions that the guns were brought into the island in Embassy diplomatic mail in contravention of the Geneva Convention.

Politics in Jamaica had never been more violent. Various estimates put the death toll from 250 to 600 during the 1980 election campaign. Despite the violence Jamaicans were clear regarding the issues confronting the electorate. First was the economic plight of the country for which much blame was ascribed to the PNP. This led to the second important issue; that of a strong desire for a change in government as it was widely believed that Manley and the PNP had introduced an element of class conflict into Jamaican politics which was seen as extremely divisive. The third issue, which was equally important, centered on the fear of communism. Although a communist takeover was highly improbable, both the JLP and the predominantly American international press gave wide coverage to this "possibility". Consequently the international community viewed the election as a contest between the United States and the Soviet Union, with Cuba acting as the latter's surrogate (Payne, 1988, pp. 67-73). Jamaicans in general did not share that view. Considerable alarm was voiced regarding Manley's close friendship with Cuba's Fidel Castro, but most Jamaicans believed that their nation would stay clear of personality based international political intrigue.

On October 30, 1980, Jamaicans, despite numerous rumors that the voting would be disrupted by the PNP, turned out in record numbers to cast their ballots. They were primarily driven to the polls because of high unemployment, empty supermarket shelves, double-digit inflation, negative foreign investment and a host of other problems. Notwithstanding the violence throughout the long campaign, the 1980 election is seen as one of the fairest and freest in Jamaica's electoral history. A record 87% of the eligible registered voters cast an all time high 853,000 votes. The JLP led by Edward Seaga won an unprecedented 59% of the popular vote to 41% for the PNP and it won fifty one of the sixty seats in the House of Representatives. Because Jamaica has a first-past-the-post rather than a proportional representation system, the party that wins the election usually has a larger majority in the House of Representatives than in the popular vote.

The landslide victory of Seaga and the JLP was considered a firm mandate for the new government. Many other observers viewed it as a strong rejection of the Manley era (Payne, 1988, p. 83). Most importantly, however, the 1980 elections demonstrated that Jamaicans are fairly committed to democracy, not the least among them Michael Manley. Manley and the PNP willingly accepted the results of the election recognizing that the people had spoken. Thus, they reinforced the democratic tradition and the entrenched two-party system which is at the core of the Jamaican political culture. The election, its results, and acceptance by all concerned demonstrated to the world community that the people of Jamaica can and do choose alternative approaches to the solution of their problems. The strength and vitality of Jamaican democracy were again demonstrated in 1989 when Manley and the PNP returned to power following victory over Seaga and the JLP in a free election.

Finally, it is very important to note that the results of the 1980 general elections in Jamaica did not pass unnoticed by the government of the United States. The United States was a key player in Jamaica's political affairs before, during, and after the events of 1980, even to the extent of actively seeking the defeat of Michael Manley and the PNP. However, the U.S. administration of President Ronald Reagan may have misinterpreted the meaning of the 1980 election as the results of Reagan's Caribbean Basin Initiative will illustrate.

Notes

1. For an insightful analysis of the Federation, see John Mordecai, *The West Indies: The Federal Negotiations*. Northwestern University Press, Evanston, 1968.

2. Hewan, Clinton G., *Politics and International Relations of the Independent West Indian Islands—Jamaica, Trinidad and Tobago, Barbados: From Colonialism to Independence*. Unpublished Masters Thesis, University of Cincinnati, 1971.

3. See Samuel J. and Edith F. Hurwitz *Jamaica: A Historical Portrait*. Praeger Publishers, New York, Washington, London, 1971.

4. Curtis A. Wilan, Ed., *The Caribbean: Contemporary Trends*, Gainesville: University of Florida Press, 1953, p. 251.

5. Ibid

6. Report of JLP Convention, November 1960 (unpublished).

7. For a full discussion of the Rodney Riots of 1968, see Anthony J. Payne *Politics in Jamaica*. C. Hurst and Co., London, St. Martin's Press, New York, 1988.

4
The State: Political and Economic Conflict

Since the early 1970s Jamaica has projected itself on the world political stage in a manner uncharacteristic of its Third World status. This has guaranteed for the island an unusual level of press coverage in the world media, especially the North American press. This special attention given Jamaica resulted initially from the high-profile pro-Cuban, and by extension pro-Soviet, foreign policy pursued by the Michael Manley administration (1972-1980). Next and of equal importance was the similarly high profile, pro United States and by inference anti-Soviet, foreign policy formulated and actively implemented by the Edward Seaga administration (1981-1989).

The belief is commonly held among Jamaicans that no other period in the nation's political history, except possibly the early post World War II era, has had a greater impact on the political and socio-economic development of the island. International and domestic political analysts who have studied this period are undecided as to whether this period should be classified as positive or negative with regard to the various development strategies with which Jamaica experimented.[1] What they have agreed is that the focus of international attention on Jamaica and its political leaders, has raised vitally important questions about the mode and character of the internal political life of Jamaica and its 2.2 million people.

This chapter addresses some of those questions with respect to the Jamaican state. It also analyzes the impact of political and economic conflict on the socio-economic structure of Jamaica and explores the relationship of those developments to the Caribbean Basin Initiative.

The State

Jamaica in varying degrees fulfills the six basic characteristics that distinguish a modern state: (1) sovereignty, that is independence from higher political authority; (2) legal equality with other states; (3) clearly defined territorial boundaries, over which it has jurisdiction; (4) diplomatic recognition by other sovereign states; (5) membership in the United Nations and other international and regional organizations; and, (6) legitimacy, that is the government is recognized as legitimate by its citizens and it enjoys their loyalty and support.

Within the context of this definition of a state there is no question that Jamaica qualifies. However, attaining this status did not follow what could be termed a traditional route. In Jamaica the abolition of slavery in 1838 and the subsequent rapid deterioration of the plantation system provided conditions that nurtured an unusually rapid increase in the size, prosperity, and political importance of the island's peasantry. The emergence of what was once a servile dispossessed group resulted in the increase of political tensions between the privileged and more powerful planter class, predominantly of European stock and seeking to preserve the status quo, and the mixed colored or brown middle class property owners who sought reform.

The freed slaves, predominantly Africans who had been deprived of all political and economic freedom and who sought these basic rights, formed a successful coalition with the brown middle class. This coalition provided the socio-political base from which emerged Jamaica's modern politics.

Jamaica, like most island nations in the Caribbean area, is a small country with a predominantly black English speaking population. Its government is a constitutional monarchy with a parliamentary democracy based on the Westminster model. While typical of the small English- speaking states of the region, this form of government is atypical to the Third World as a whole.

Jamaica has had a long history of economic, cultural and political links with Western Europe and North America. It has also been greatly influenced by the form of capitalism found in the countries in these two regions. Jamaica enjoys a middle income status (per capita GDP in 1985 was U.S. $940) within the Third World.[2] It is fully incorporated into the world capitalist system as a supplier of agricultural exports, a source of minerals, a tourist resort area, a major supplier of cheap labor and migrants, and a heavy consumer of Western culture and commodity exports.

As one of the former British colonies granted independence in the post-World War II period, Jamaica inherited a Western European (primarily British) type of constitution. The constitution provided for an elected parliamentary government, competitive political parties, civil rights and liberties, and a judicial system based on the common law traditions of Great Britain. Under this democratic system of government, administrative and executive power is vested in the hands of the prime minister and his cabinet, who are accountable to the lower house of the legislature, the House of Representatives. The lower house consists of sixty representatives elected in single-member constituencies to five-year terms. The upper house of the Bicameral legislature, consists of a Senate of twenty one members appointed by the governor general. Thirteen of these members are appointed on the advice of the prime minister, while eight are appointed on the advice of the leader of the opposition.

The 1962 constitution consists of 138 articles in ten basic chapters. The clauses of the constitution may be amended by a two-thirds majority in both houses of Parliament, or in the case that the upper house, the Senate, does not concur, amendment may be achieved with the approval of a special majority of the electorate voting in a referendum.

The judicial system, which forms an intricate part of the state apparatus functions on an independent basis. Memers of the high court and the appellate judiciary enjoy security of tenure and are protected from political or any other state-related form of interference. The judiciary is headed by a Supreme Court holding both primary and appellate jurisdiction. Members of both the Supreme Court and the Court of Appeals are appointed by the Governor General on the advice of the Prime Minister

Having opted to remain an independent member of the Commonwealth, Jamaica retains the Queen of England as its chief of state. Executive power is vested nominally in the Queen but exercised by the Governor General, whom the Queen appoints on the recommendation of the Prime Minister. Finally, individual rights and freedoms are explicitly subject to respect for the rights of others and the public interest in matters of defense, order, health, and morality.

Within the context of modern democratic traditions, the Jamaican state is firmly grounded. Strenuous efforts have been made to ensure that the rights of the citizen are in harmony with the responsibilities of state authority. Through universal suffrage and the domination of the vote by the two major political parties a large representative cross section of the citizenry has been incorporated into the governing structure. This has resulted in a stable society. Consequently, there has been a remarkable continuity in institutional forms between the early aristocratic state and the later reformed democratic state that has developed along the lines of British parliamentary government.

A troubling question emerges, however, regarding the high level of political violence experienced in Jamaica since independence, particularly in the 1970s and early 1980s. This phenomenon, one should note, belies the democratic structures and processes evident in the established state institutions. Of equal concern is the changing mode of political consciousness and activism within the various classes, especially the majority working class. An analysis of these phenomena will facilitate understanding of Jamaica's political culture and of why the island experiences sporadic but intense political tensions.

The political system in Jamaica has had to cope with many crises in the post-independence period. Of considerable note is the severe economic crisis of the 1970s and 1980s along with the extreme negative political conflicts that were the products of that crisis. The crisis management techniques utilized by successive governments, have in the opinion of some analysts, influenced substantially the character of Jamaican democracy.[3] These crises have also highlighted the impact and tenure of external influence on the domestic and foreign affairs of the island. We proceed, then, to examine the causes and effects of political conflict in Jamaica since independence.

Political Conflict 1974-1980

As noted in Chapter Three the changes in leadership of the political parties in Jamaica, beginning with the JLP in 1966 and followed by the PNP in 1969, signalled the first indication of an impending ideological shift. This ideological shift, however, did not emerge suddenly. Between 1966, when Donald Sangster took over as leader of the JLP only to be succeeded by Hugh Shearer after Sangster's death in 1967, and 1969 when Michael Manley assumed leadership of the PNP, the two parties pursued similar centrist policies. Both sought the support of all classes, accepted a reformist position on public policy that gave vital backing to private business while supporting government spending in the area of social needs, and shared a common view of foreign policy, especially with regard to links with Western Europe and the United States.

Relations between the two parties during the period 1969 to 1972 were generally agreeable due in part to the excellent personal relations that existed between Michael Manley and Hugh Shearer. However, some differences did exist. The PNP, prior to assuming the leadership of government in 1972, was a typical social-democratic party. That is, it was a party content with capitalism and private ownership while seeking to achieve programs conducive to social reform. In contrast, the JLP demonstrated the attributes of a typical Caribbean trade union based party, avoiding any extremes in ideology while embracing pragmatic reforms that responded to the social needs of the unionized worker as well as the peasant. While the PNP sought to justify the need for active state involvement in the management of the economy, the JLP demonstrated a strong faith in the unrestricted operation of the market economy. Its position endorsed a more orthodox capitalist system embracing a dominant private sector (Stone, 1986, pp. 151-52).

Despite the apparently tranquil relations between the political parties tension was very much evident in the political arena. By the time general elections were held in 1972 the articulated positions regarding party philosophy clearly revealed fundamental differences that had developed beneath the surface. The JLP based its campaign on the strength of the economy its policies had built since assuming office in 1962. The prosperity of the 1960s proved to be an insufficient incentive to the voters who were more concerned with the unemployment level and with the manifestly unequal distribution of the nation's wealth. The JLP had to contend with the growing appeal of the PNP's populist politics promising a more equal distribution of wealth.

On the strength of its populist politics as well as a general dissatisfaction with the JLP, Michael Manley and the PNP won the 1972 general elections ending a decade of JLP government. The PNP won thirty seven of the fifty three seats in the House of Representatives, with what was at that time a record 56% of the popular vote. Skillfully utilizing populist themes such as "the word is love" and "power to the people", Manley was able to convince a wide cross section of Jamaicans that his policies could offer greater socio-economic justice and continued economic prosperity.

Assuming control of the government at the beginning of the nation's second decade of independence Michael Manley appeared as a very attractive alternative to Hugh Shearer. To many Jamaicans in 1972, Manley and the PNP held out the promise of an end to the hardships they had endured since independence. Manley was, in the opinion of many, the first political leader to make Jamaicans fully realize that they were capable of controlling their country's destiny and thereby of significantly changing its political and economic structures.

In the opinion of many political analysts, the emergence of the PNP as the governing party in 1972 marked a major turning point in Jamaica's modern political history. John D. Forbes in his analysis of the period argues that the skillful public relations and campaign promises of Michael Manley led to an extremely high level of popular expectations. This rising level of expectation eventually led in part to Manley's demise. Due to many circumstances, some of his doing and others arising from external sources completely out of his control, he subsequently failed to live up to what the country had been led to believe he could accomplish (Forbes, 1986, p. 17).

The Manley era, 1972-1980, saw an unprecedented level of political tension, external political and economic interference primarily from the United States, and a high level of polititization among the electorate not experienced previously in Jamaica. Although there are numerous explanations of these developments, there is one common thread that ties them together; that is Michael Manley's experimentation with democratic socialism. It is therefore necessary in view of the importance of this concept and the fundamental role that it played in the politics of the 1970s to explore its effects on the political economy of Jamaica.

Democratic Socialism and Domestic/Economic Policy

In September 1974 the PNP government announced at the party's 36th Annual Conference that the party and the government had converted to socialism. The announcement was made in a speech by Prime Minister Manley. Until then the initiatives of the PNP government (1972-1974) had been welcomed in most sectors of society and the economy. Growth in the public sector was steady. This was evident in expenditures as well as direct employment. The results of the government's policies were evident in agriculture in the form of a modest land redistribution program. The state had by then become the owner of most public utilities including transportation and a number of previously privately owned businesses. Prior to Manley's announcement the rhetoric and actions of the government were fully consistent with the views and expectations of a large segment of the population. This general acceptance of government policy muted somewhat the objections of those in opposition. Manley and the PNP were beyond any doubt fully in control and overwhelmingly accepted by the people.

The declaration of Democratic Socialism and the program unveiled afterwards attracted worldwide attention and set the stage for one of the most intense political debates ever witnessed in Jamaica. This debate involved every segment of society and focused PNP policies on the problems of development and social change. Although some analysts have argued that the PNP "converted" to socialism in 1974, the reality is that socialism formed the basis of the PNP from its founding. The now famous August 20, 1940 statement by the party founder, Norman Manley, and the subsequent internal upheaval of 1952 involving the "Four H's", Ken and Frank Hill, Richard Hart and Arthur

Henry will attest to that fact.[4]

Michael Manley's restatement of the PNP commitment to socialism and the reasons why the party felt it necessary to again embrace that ideology were conditioned by their claims of flexibility and an undoctrinaire acceptance of the "equality of man" anchored in the knowledge that "human beings are moral and capable of acting together to achieve common purposes."[5] Despite the foregoing, which many viewed as an attempt to placate the electorate, a sizable portion of the electorate registered real doubts and in some cases fear as to the true meaning of the party's new departure. Manley and the PNP initially responded to such concerns through simplifications. It employed various catch phrases such as "Socialism is Christianity in Action," or that "Socialism Says no man shall be allowed to exploit his brother," to define and explain democratic socialism and attract support for it. This attempt failed or succeeded depending on whether one supported the party or not.

Manley attempted to fill in the details of the new program in a speech to the House of Representatives on November 20, 1974 by outlining the party's concept of a mixed economy. Interestingly, he also revealed that early in its history the PNP had declared itself a socialist party. In a further attempt to allay the fears of the Jamaican people and those of important external interests, the PNP released a document entitled "Democratic Socialism the Jamaican Model". Payne maintains that as a manifesto the document turned out to be "a sophisticated and skillful piece of special pleading" (Payne, 1987, p. 36). He noted also that readers were informed that "many Governments throughout the world are attempting to devise methods of organizing the citizens of their nations so that everyone has equal opportunities. This search has led people finally to Socialism—the only system of social and economic organization that is designed to make opportunities equal and open to all" (Payne, 1987, p. 36).

Jamaicans in general and foreign business and political interests in particular were not terribly impressed with the PNP's concept of socialism. To many political and economic analysts such as Anthony Payne and the team of Evelyn and John Stephens, the contents of the manifesto offered no credible program of action in that no targets were specified, nor were there any stated procedures for policy implementation. Rather, the manifesto was a statement of progressive moral and philosophical goals persuasively argued, but seriously marred by "excessive simplifications". While the document did not adequately fullfil the definition of a philosophical treatise, its message as Payne argued, was very clear in that the PNP proposed a reform of capitalism in an effort to make it work to the advantage of the ordinary people (Payne, 1987, p. 37).

Although the document was neither original nor particularly radical in content, reactions to it assumed from the domestic and foreign business communities and from the Nixon administration were predictably negative. Supporters of the PNP along with prominent members of the party argued that the adverse reactions to the contents of the manifesto were aimed at discrediting the party's policies and programmes in an effort to maintain the status quo. In their view this was neo-colonialist exploitation.

On closer examination of the PNP manifesto it becomes clear that the adverse reactions to its contents may in fact have been excessively harsh. Indeed the document lacked detail on the question of a mixed economy. Regarding the method by which the country would achieve socialism, it noted there was no "single road which a nation must follow to create a socialist society. Each nation must work out its methods of solving its own problems and meeting the basic needs of its people."[6] In response to a persistent rumor that the party intended to turn Jamaica into a communist state, the manifesto stated that the party had "no intention of blindly copying any foreign formula for achieving a Socialist society in Jamaica." Rather it was "constructing our own model of Socialism, which must grow out of the application of basic principles to the special nature of Jamaican society."[7]

Even prior to the reaffirmation of socialism as an ideological model of development for Jamaica, Michael Manley had written that "the first task that a post-colonial society must tackle is the development of a strategy designed to replace the psychology of dependence with the spirit of individual and collective self-reliance. Until that exercise is successfully embarked upon every other plan will fail." Manley demonstrated an uncanny grasp of the need for fundamental change and the importance of self-reliance as a motivating factor by adding, "Indeed without the spirit of self-reliance, it is doubtful if a successful indigenous plan can be devised; instead time and energy may be dissipated in the adoption of other people's plans, designed for other situations, to solve other people's problems" (Manley, 1974, p. 15).

The foregoing analysis should help to clarify the ideas and intentions behind Manley's and the PNP's socialist rhetoric. It is clear that neither advocated a program of wide-ranging nationalization of foreign owned enterprises or the wholesale elimination of the private sector. Rather, as Payne noted, the dominant theme was that of partnership with existing ownership" (Payne, 1988, p. 39). Reactions from foreign capitals such as Washington and the subsequent implementation of policies by succeeding governments of the United States between 1974 to 1980 aimed at frustrating the PNP's plans were excessive and thus contributed to the rise of political conflict in Jamaica.

On the one hand, it can be argued that Michael Manley and the PNP made serious policy mistakes such as alienating the business sector, or making what some considered threatening statements regarding the affluent in pursuit of social changes in Jamaica. Moreover, these actions led to the eventual demise of democratic socialism as a viable vehicle for change. On the other hand, there is evidence to substantiate a widely accepted belief that Manley was the first post-independence leader of Jamaica to instill in the people a feeling that they could control their country's destiny and that they could significantly restructure the economic and social system that they inherited from colonialism. He sought to reset the psychological tone of the society by stressing self-reliance, indulging in the ritualistic clearing away of some of the symbols of the colonial and neo-colonial eras and appealing to Jamaicans to produce more of what they consume. Despite impressive economic growth between the years 1962 to 1972 most Jamaicans were genuinely dissatisfied with their society, especially with respect to the distribution of wealth. Almost immediately after assuming office, the Manley government restored a number of civil liberties, issued passports to people long denied that basic privilege, and abolished entry bans on many publications considered left-wing.

In the area of foreign relations, trade and diplomatic ties were established with many socialist countries including Cuba. Jamaica made it clear that it fully identified with the aspirations of the Third World and it spared no effort to condemn political, economic and social repression such as that manifested under a system of apartheid and racism.

One of the big problems Manley had to confront in the early stages of his administration was the resolution of the question of the distribution of economic power. His recognition of this fundamental problem was clearly reflected in his book, *The Politics of Change*:

> It is impossible to modify the distribution of wealth without considering the ownership of resources. Where the means of production are concentrated in a few hands, it is inevitable that wealth will tend to accumulate in those hands at the expense of the rest of the population (Manley, 1974, p. 88).

Manley insisted that the system of ownership of the island's economy should "be consistent with national objectives," and noted that the nation's "resources must be controlled to ensure that they are used to the full and in a manner consistent with social justice" (Manley, 1974, p. 89). Pointing to the fact that the "Commanding heights"[8] of the Jamaican economy were almost totally under the control of foreign interests, Manley argued "that political independence and foreign economic domination of strategic sectors of the economy are mutually exclusive concepts" (Manley, 1975, p. 115). Also, he condemned the developmental strategy which forms the basis of the Puerto Rican model of "industrialization by invitation" embraced by the JLP government during the 1960s.

In its efforts to have the people of Jamaica better understand the philosophy underlying democratic socialism and the changes this ideology proposes to make in the society the PNP government cited a number of policy mistakes and weakness of the previous JLP government. It paid particular attention to the flawed nature of the Jamaicanization program, especially its inability to correct, as Manley noted, the "oligarchic pattern of ownership of local resources." He further observed that "the tendency has been for the same wealthy minority to buy into the newly offered equity and no effective program has been devised for spreading the base of equity holding further to a conscious program of democratization of the ownership of resources" (Manley, 1974, p. 100).

This external control coupled with foreign attempts at acquisition of equity under the existing system of ownership would, Manley believed, almost certainly lead to unacceptable pressures on Jamaica's balance of payments and limited foreign reserves. The attempts to resolve the redistribution of economic wealth problem, the psychological reorientation of society to enable the people to cope with the vestiges of colonialism, and Manley's approach to the redefinition of Jamaica's foreign policy within the context of a Third World experience provides some indication of the specific aims of the PNP government in its attempt to reform Jamaican society. Not surprising were adverse internal and external reactions to the concept and implementation of Democratic Socialism, such as the fears that heightened political and economic awareness would threaten the existence of the established order and that the reordering of Jamaica's foreign relations would negatively affect the regional geopolitical status quo. Such reactions by those forces opposed to the new order led to their efforts to control the trends that they perceived.

Democratic Socialism and Foreign Policy

If it can be said that local and general foreign reactions to the domestic and economic policies of the PNP government, as embodied in the ideology of democratic socialism, were excessive the following analysis of the government's foreign policy will show that the responeses of the Nixon, Ford, and Carter administrations were even more disproportionate.

As stated in Chapter Three Michael Manley and the PNP government did make a number of tactical mistakes and some basic errors of judgement. One is forced to conclude, however, that Manley and his government allowed themselves to be outmanuevered by the opposition, Edward Seaga and the JLP whose leadership Seaga assumed in 1974, and most importantly the United States beginning with the Nixon administration in 1974. Finding itself politically and economically pressured, due in part to occasional mishandling of some policy issues which worked to the benefit of both the JLP and the United States, the PNP in a desperate effort to extricate itself from what many Jamaicans and some foreign observes saw as a self-inflicted dilemma succeeded only in becoming more entangled in the web of superpower intrigue.

Whether Michael Manley and the PNP recognized it or not, and there is no evidence to suggest that they did not, the espousal of "Democratic Socialism" and a steadfast commitment to its ideology would propel Jamaica into the probing glare of the international spotlight with serious superpower political and economic overtones. More than any other country in the Caribbean, except on brief occasions for Guyana, Jamaica took international center stage in the 1970s. During the eight and one half years of the PNP administration (1972-1980) Jamaica moved from the status of a relatively obscure former colony to an active participant in superpower politics. "The whole Manley experiment" as Payne observed "constitutes dramatic evidence of the problems and possibilities that attach to 'democratic socialist' strategies of reform in trying to overcome dependence in the Third World" (Payne, 1988, p. 60).[9] (This condition has of course, changed with the easing of the cold war and the collapse of communism).

In 1972 when the PNP assumed leadership of the government of Jamaica the island's economy had become complex and diverse. The economy had also become, however, increasingly dependent on external forces. The rapid expansion in all sectors of the economy were based primarily on foreign private capital primarily from the United States and to a lesser extent Canada. The controlling impact of U.S. capital was very much evident in manufacturing, tourism, the bauxite industry, and most major financial institutions. The result of this extensive U.S. and Canadian investment was the gradual shift of Jamaica from a Western European sphere of influence to one dominated by North

America. As Payne summarized the situation, "within a decade of independence Jamaica had been effectively transferred from British colonial control into the less overt but still highly effective domain of U.S. hemispheric power" (Payne, 1988, p. 61).

This shift of the control of the Jamaican economy into a U.S. dominated sphere sharply influenced the structure and composition of the nation's class system. One important result of this shift was the growth of a domestic managerial class controlled by North American interests and devoid of any real power in shaping the nation's economic destiny. Whatever semblance of power or control this group exercised came about as a result of a subordinate "middle man" relationship with foreign firms. This subordinate position involved all areas of business operations; financing, management, marketing, and planning. In short, Jamaica's economy was heavily dependent on foreign entities whose interests were not necessarily congruent with those of the island. Recognizing this state of affairs, Manley made it one of his priorities to create an economy that would be less susceptible to foreign control.

The creation of a less dependent economy necessitated, in Manley's view, the extension of state control into the "commanding heights" of the Jamaican economy. Although the PNP administration advocated complete government ownership of public utilities, it recognized that both public ownership and private capital would have to work together especially in areas such as bauxite, banking, tourism, and sugar. Manley rejected outright expropriation knowing the negative impact it would have on the supply of investment capital, both foreign and domestic, for the nation's economy. Indeed he argued that "the question is not whether to use foreign capital in development planning but how to bring it into harmony with national aspirations". But he qualified his willingness to rely on foreign investment by noting three prime considerations: its price; its potential impact on Jamaican control of economic decision-making; and the purposes for which it would be used (Manley, 1974, p. 117).

In proposing a foreign policy commensurate with the needs and aspirations of Jamaica, Manley articulated the belief that the nation's foreign policy "begins with the perception of self interest." The initiatives undertaken by his government prescribed a change, an independent "third path" for Jamaica, the rest of the Caribbean and indeed all of the Third World. In keeping with its independent foreign policy the PNP administration rejected both the Puerto Rican and Cuban models of development. The former it regarded as a proven ineffective method, the latter it viewed as based on a Marxist ideology which is alien to the Jamaican way of thinking and the nation's past experience. Both models of development were also rejected because of their heavy dependence on one of the superpowers. Manley pointedly noted that it was "self-evident to us that we want to be pawns neither of East nor West, economically or politically" (Manley, 1982, p. 221).

The concept of an open and independent foreign policy purused by a the Manley government included non-alignment, strong and active support of Third World initiatives especially in the areas of economic and political freedom, and the promotion of a new international economic order that would be favorable to developing countries. Manley pointedly argued that when the question of defining an open foreign policy arises Jamaica wishes "to establish the fact that the entire world is the stage upon which a country, however small pursues this perception of self-interest" (Manley, 1974, p. 144). The emphasis on lessening Jamaica's dependence on North America and Western Europe, along with the reordering of the international economic system was of critical importance to the new foreign policy thrust. It also demonstrated an international dimension to Manley's program of change. The underlying basis of this change was the belief that reform in the domestic sphere would be possible only if the government could negotiate better terms for Jamaica in every aspect of its dealings with the international economic community.

With this very important policy initiative firmly in mind, the Manley government sought to meet some of its economic objectives by bringing industries such as sugar and bauxite partially under public control. Such action understandably was viewed as a radical redirecting of Jamaica's post-independence foreign policy by foreign economic interests who felt threatened by the Manley government. These initiatives, however, should more correctly be viewed as the legitimate actions of a sovereign independent nation. As an integral part of the Third World, Jamaica attached much importance to the concept of collective self-reliance. It held that Third World nations should begin to assert greater control over their natural resources as well as determine for themselves what is in their best interests.

In demonstrating the seriousness of his government's new foreign policy, Manley proposed the creation of an International Bauxite Association (IBA), a cartel that would in some ways patterned after OPEC. He succeeded in this venture when in February 1974 the association comprising the major bauxite producers was formed at a conference in Conakry, Guinea. The constitution of the IBA carefully excluded any attempt to use bauxite as a political weapon as in the case of OPEC. The association's terms of reference include matters vitally important to the member countries such as the exchange of information, co-operation in the development of government strategies, and a statement of a general intention to acquire maximum national control and ownership of the bauxite industry in each of the member territories. In reality the IBA is an organization whose primary aim is to help member countries "to act for their mutual benefit in the economic field" (Manley, 1974, p. 255).

The creation of the IBA was not the only international policy success of the Manley government in its quest for Third World collective self-reliance. Also significant was the establishment of the Third World Development Fund under joint Kuwaiti-Jamaican sponsorship. In addition, Jamaica adopted an open foreign policy which encouraged relations with a wide variety of countries irrespective of political systems and ideology. These contacts were mostly outside the island's traditional group of friends. The international community received notice that Jamaica would support wars of liberation in Africa. This, however, was not a new policy, or as opponents of the Manley government would argue, a radical departure from the norm. The fact is that since independence Jamaica supported liberation movements in Africa, if not materially then certainly rhetorically. Indeed previous JLP governments refused to have any relations with South Africa, Rhodesia and Portugal because of the racist and oppressive policies of the governments of those countries.

The U.S. Reacts to the Manley Government

The major problems of the Manley government in its relations with the United States government began as a result of two significant foreign policy initiatives undertaken by Manley. First, as noted earlier, Manley was instrumental in the creation of the International Bauxite Association. His relentless efforts in forming the IBA drew the attention of Washington. Bauxite is an important strategic mineral. Jamaica was at that time supplying approximately half of the U. S. requirement (Sherry and Girling, 1978, p. 19). Although Manley sought to explain Jamaica's position personally to Secretary of state Henry Kissinger, the U.S. government strongly opposed the formation of the IBA because "this touched a raw American nerve in that it purported to promote a wider Third World resistance to Western economic interests" (Payne, 1988, p. 70). Collective self-reliance embodying the control of a country's natural resources was at the root of Manley's policies and should have been understood as such. However, it aroused the hostility of the U. S.

The second foreign policy initiative was in fact two-pronged. Soon after winning the 1972 general election the Manley government and the governments of the other independent Commonwealth Caribbean countries established full diplomatic relations with Cuba. The U. S. ambassador to Jamaica made known his displeasure at this move and blamed Manley for having encouraged the other Caribbean leaders to establish relations with the Fidel Castro government. The second aspect of the initiative involved the 1973 non-aligned summit meeting in Algiers. Manley was invited by Cuba's Castro to fly to the conference with Castro in his private plane. Manley incurred the wrath of the U. S. and the Jamaican opposition for doing so. The greatest resentment, however, resulted from a speech Manley gave at the non-aligned conference offering to raise volunteers in the Caribbean "to fight in any capacity in the various wars of liberation" in Africa, "provided the African peoples involved could finance the volunteers and find useful tasks for them" (Manley, 1975, p. 256). The foregoing, coupled with a strong push for support of a "New International Economic Order," began a series of events that would lead inexorably to worsening relations with the U. S.

The real turning point in relations with the U.S. came in 1974 when the Manley government informed the general public that it intended to begin renegotiating the tax agreements signed with U.S. and Canadian bauxite and alumina companies. These agreements had not been changed in any way or form since the early 1950s when, as Payne noted, "the industry was first set up in Jamaica and produced only a token tax yield for the government" (Payne, 1988, p. 68). Contrary to the belief held in Washington, the effects of the severe economic crisis at the time rather than a political commitment, forced Manley to push ahead with the renegotiations. Jamaica's economy was unable to cope with the impact of the sudden rise in oil prices and the world wide economic recession that resulted from it. In one year, 1973-1974, Jamaica's oil import bill increased from J$65 million to approximately J$177 million.[10]

The cost of other essential imports rose, especially food and manufactured goods, adding to the existing pressure on the cost of living and the balance of payments. External capital investment and income from tourism declined. These developments coupled with a dramatic increase in state expenditures forced Manley to seek an increase in revenues from the most logical source, bauxite. Following several months of inconclusive talks, in which the bauxite companies employed various blocking tactics to frustrate the efforts of the government, Manley abrogated the agreements and proceed to "impose a novel method of raising revenue" (Payne, 1988, p. 68). Manley was aware of the potential consequences of his action. Prior to the start of talks with the bauxite companies Manley visited Canadian Prime Minister Pierre Trudeau and U.S. Secretary of State Henry Kissinger to fully appraise them of the reasons for the bauxite talks and most importantly to assure them that the policies and actions of Jamaica in regard to the bauxite negotiations implied no political hostility toward Canada or the U. S. (Manley, 1974, pp. 259-60).

Following the meetings with Trudeau and Kissinger, meetings were held with the presidents of the bauxite corporations to explain the government's new policies. Despite these strenuous efforts, Manley noted "that the corporations did not understand that we were serious and were reluctant to admit to the reasonableness of our case." He further stated, "we were asking for an increase in tax revenue which would have added, if passed fully on to the consumer, 6 per cent to the price of aluminum ingot. We were seeking this when we had been required to pay more than 200 per cent increase for wheat" (Manley, 1975, p. 260).[11] Thus in a unilateral action Jamaica imposed the new tax by legislation. The new tax in the form of a "levy" would be imposed on all bauxite mined and processed in the island. The levy was "set at 7 1/2 percent of the selling price of the aluminum ingot instead of a tax assessed according to an artificial profit level negotiated between the companies and the government" (Payne, 1988, pp. 68-69).

The bauxite industry is of significant importance to the economy of Jamaica. The industry represents as Manley noted "the largest single capital investment, earns the most foreign exchange and pays the most taxes of any industry in the Island." This, however, is tempered by the fact as Manley further noted that the industry "is exclusively under foreign ownership and control, processes less than half of its mining output to the alumina stage of the aluminum process and has established no major aluminum fabricating complex in Jamaica" (Manley, 1974, p. 113).[12] From the PNP government's perspective, the bauxite levy was an extremely effective mechanism for ensuring a fair return to the treasury of revenue that was necessary for helping to build a sound economic base. The new revenue brought an added J$147.63 million, reflecting a rise in revenue from J$22.71 million in 1972 to J$170.34 million in 1974.[13]

The Manley government received the support of the majority of the Jamaican people on the bauxite question. They had always regarded the foreign owners of the industry as greedy and not at all interested in the welfare of the people of Jamaica (Manley, 1974, pp. 258-62). Many share the belief of Norman Girvan that the Caribbean bauxite industry is a classic case of economic imperialism." Only a part of the value of the industry's 'sales' actually accrue to the Caribbean economies; and only an infinitesimal fraction of the value of the end products flows back to the Caribbean people" (Girvan, 1976, pp. 99-100. Even the "Jamaican Capitalist Class" (Payne, 1988, p. 69) gave much enthusiastic support to the new bauxite policy, and as Payne observed "their role was recognized by the appointment of two leading members of the class, Meyer Matalon and Patrick Rousseau, as chairman and vice-chairman respectively of the National Bauxite Commission, which presided over the negotiations with the companies" (Payne, 1988, p. 69).

The imposition of the new bauxite levy signalled only the start of a series of initiatives on the part of government to secure more revenue from the industry. The "bauxite offensive" included talks with the companies regarding the acquisition of majority control in their local operations. It also included the formation of the Jamaican Bauxite Institute to provide the government with independent data on the technical aspects of the industry. The initial response of the aluminum corporations to the government's actions was one of open hostility. A suit contesting the legality of the levy was filed with the International Center for the Settlement of Investment Disputes, a division of the World Bank. Simultaneously the government of the United States was urged to intervene on behalf of the corporations with the government of Jamaica, while a massive transfer of bauxite and alumina production from Jamaica to other countries was undertaken. As a result of these retaliatory moves, Jamaica's share of the world bauxite market plummeted from 19% to an all time low of under 14% between the years 1973 and 1976. During the same period the share of Australia and Guinea increased substantially.[14]

The bauxite companies, despite their public posturing, eventually reached an accommodation with the government of Jamaica.[15] They realized continued access to Jamaica's bauxite would necessitate a set of new tactics appropriate to the rapidly changing times. They were also very much aware of the fact that many of their alumina plants were specifically geared to Jamaican ore, and as such it would prove extremely costly to redesign them. The companies also had to accept the government's joint venture proposal, wherein the government of Jamaica purchased all the land owned by the companies in Jamaica as well as 51 percent of the mining operations in the Island. In the final analysis, the government's challenge to the position of the bauxite companies appears as Payne argued "rather more muted", because the companies retained the refining plants as well as management control for a minimum of ten years from the time the agreement was signed. Finally, as Payne further noted, in "the unspoken part of the agreements" the companies "also maintained their superiority in technology, control of the market and access to capital" (Payne, 1988, p. 70).

Thus, it can be argued that the concessions won by the Manley government in its struggle with the bauxite multinational corporations were really shallow ones.

In the long term, the struggle between the Manley government and the bauxite industry may have been a costly one for the government. This is because the United States began to view Manley and his policies as contrary to its interests and therefore a threat to the security of the United States. As noted earlier bauxite is a mineral of strategic importance to the United States. Consequently, Manley's willingness to confront the exploitive practices of the bauxite companies coupled with his relentless efforts to form a cartel of bauxite producing countries had, in the view of U.S. foreign policy makers, gone too far. Manley and his Democratic Socialism had become a threat to U.S. national security and, moreover they "purported to promote a wider Third World resistance to Western economic interests" (Payne, 1988, p. 70). Manley's increasingly friendly relations with Cuba including an historic official visit to Havana in which he made his now famous anti-imperialist speech did not help the situation. Manley's actions, legitimate as they were, generated real if unfounded doubts within the decision making circles of Washington. Manley finally dropped what in the eyes of Washington was the biggest bomb of all when he announced his government's support of the decision of the government of Cuba to send troops to assist Angolans in their struggle against a U.S. and South African supported faction opposed to the Marxist government in that country. The Cuban decision to send troops came only after South African troops moved into Angolan territory assisted by the U.S. Central Intelligence Agency(CIA).

Apparently it was immaterial to the U.S. government that Manley's decision to support the sending of Cuban troops to Angola, "despite a clear warning from Henry Kissinger" not to do so (Payne, 1988, p. 71), was in keeping with traditional Jamaican policy. Succeeding governments since Jamaica attained independence had vehemently condemned the racist policies of Portugal and South Africa as well as the former Smith regime in Rhodesia (now Zimbabwe). Furthermore, "The announcement was made out of a sense of morality that typified Manley's approach to international relations" (Payne, 1988, p. 71). Morality and an abhorrence of racism displayed by the Manley government notwithstanding, the U.S. government halted economic aid to Jamaica (later reinstated on a limited basis by the Carter administration). This punitive action led eventually to the severe decline of Jamaica's economy. (See table 4.1). This brought in its wake some of the harshest times witnessed by Jamaicans since the great depression of the 1930s and the World War II years 1939

TABLE 4.1 U.S. Loans and and Grants to Jamaica, 1956-82 (U.S. fiscal years—U.S. $ millions—new obligations)

	Annual average 1956-60	Annual average 1961-5	Annual average 1966-70	1971	1972	1973	1974	1975	1976[a]	1977	1978	1979	1980	1981	1982
Economic Assistance – total	1.0	5.3	3.7	23.1	6.1	8.4	13.2	4.3	5.1	32.2	23.3	18.1	14.6	73.5	138.6
AID	0.2	3.1	1.0	20.9	1.2	5.6	9.9	0.6	0.9	17.5	11.6	6.0	2.7	53.9	119.4
(Security Supporting Assist.)[a]	( )	( )	( )	( )	( )	( )	( )	( )	( )	( )	(11.0)	( )	( )	(41.0)	(90.5)
	0.8	1.9	2.1	1.1	3.9	1.4	1.8	1.6	2.6	13.4	10.5	10.2	10.0	17.1	17.5
Food for Peace															
Other Economic Assistance[b]	–	0.3	0.7	1.1	1.0	1.4	1.5	2.1	1.6	1.2	1.2	1.9	1.9	2.5	1.7
Military Assistance – total	–	0.1	0.1	–	–	–	–	–	–	–	–	–	–	1.7	2.1
Total economic and military	1.0	5.4	3.8	23.1	6.1	8.4	13.2	4.3	5.1	32.2	23.3	18.1	14.6	75.1	140.7
Loans	–	2.3	–	20.0	–	4.4	9.9	1.4	2.4	28.5	19.5	12.7	10.0	69.4	129.4
Grants	1.0	3.1	3.8	3.1	6.1	4.0	3.3	2.9	2.7	3.7	3.8	5.4	4.6	5.8	11.3
Other US Loans[c]	–	0.9	5.6	0.9	17.5	7.3	15.9	16.1	0.2	0.5	–	–	–	7.4	1.5
Ex-Im Loans	–	0.9	5.6	0.9	16.7	7.3	15.9	16.1	0.2	–	–	–	–	6.4	–
All other	–	–	–	–	0.8	–	–	–	–	0.5	–	–	–	1.0	1.5

NOTES
(a) Includes Economic Support Fund
(b) Includes $3m grant by the Inter-American Foundation
(c) Represents Private Trade Agreements under Title I, PL 480 and OPIC direct loan.
(d) Includes transitional quarter.

SOURCE AID (1983).

through 1945.

The decision of the U.S. to undertake a systematic undermining of the Jamaican economy exemplifies U.S. foreign policy toward the Caribbean in general and Jamaica in particular during the 1970s. That policy, in all its varied forms, entails U.S. efforts to shape and control "the overall dynamics of the broader political and economic development in Jamaica during the PNP period in office" (Stephens and Stephens, 1986, p. 81). Geopolitical considerations, such as the spread of Marxist-Lennism by Cuba, added to the deterioration in U.S. Jamaican relations. Manley's actions in expressing support for Castro played into the hands of the United States and its willing ally, the Jamaican capitalist class. The PNP's public espousal of socialism and the broadening scope of Jamaican foreign policy, especially in advocating solidarity with Cuba's "armed adventurism," aroused the fears and anxiety of that class and resulted in its open hostility to Manley and the PNP. Domestic and international opponents of Manley began to cooperate in the task of deposing Manley and the PNP government. Vigorous "Democratic Socialism" and the new independent Third World-oriented foreign policy marked the limit of the PNP's acceptability to the members of the Jamaican capitalist class and the government of the U.S. (Payne, 1988, p. 71).

The PNP's public espousal of a socialist path to development hit on a sensitive nerve not only with regard to the capitalist class, but surprisingly that of a large segment of Jamaicans. Indeed it can be argued that the opposition to the Manley government, especially after 1974, covered the entire socio-political spectrum involving large numbers of previous supporters of the PNP. The greatest damage, however, resulted from the reaction of the capitalist class to socialism and, as Payne has noted "it fed a long standing suspicion of ideas within Jamaican political culture, which the business sector fully shared". This heightened the fear of the business sector because in their way of thinking "socialism" threatened to arouse among the masses too great a sense of their latent power. In short, "socialism seemed to open all sorts of doors behind which the specter of revolution had hitherto been conveniently locked" (Payne, 1988, pp. 71-72).

The championing of democratic socialism by the Manley government resulted in the coming together of three basic opposition groups whose sole aim was the defeat of Manley and his policies. At the forefront were the U. S., along with the local Jamaican capitalist class and the Jamaica Labor Party (JLP). Working in tandem they succeeded in exerting an enormous amount of political and economic pressure that brought the Jamaican economy to a standstill. The local business class showed its dislike for the Manley government by engaging in a systematic reduction of their investments in Jamaica. This action was closely followed by the illegal export of large amounts of foreign currency. There also occurred the largest mass migration of professional and ordinary Jamaicans to the United States since World War II.

Those opposing the Manley regime who were unable or unwilling to leave Jamaica, set about creating an element of fear and panic which helped to bring the corporate economy to a virtual standstill. The Manley government responded in early 1976 by charging the United States with undertaking a systematic campaign of 'destabilization' against Jamaica. Manley charged that the campaign was being planned and executed by local and foreign forces and he argued that "destabilization describes a situation where some source either inside or outside a country or perhaps two sources working in concert, one outside and one inside set out to create a situation of instability and panic by design" (Manley, 1982, p. 138). Indeed Manley's charge was not as far off base as some have argued.[16] The events in Chile in 1973, as revealed in subsequent Senate hearings, were similar to those events in Jamaica.

Charges that the United States had adopted a destabilization policy aimed at Jamaica came to light for the first time in early 1976. Senior members of the PNP party and high ranking members of the government including Manley claimed that "a systematic campaign was being waged by local and foreign forces against their very right to govern" (Payne, 1988, p. 50). They pointed to the similarities between the experience of Allende in Chile and that of Manley and his government in Jamaica, including the repeated denials coming from senior State Department officials. While strenuous efforts were made not to directly accuse the U.S. government, it became patently clear that Jamaica was indeed being destabilized.[17] Eventually, Minister of National Security Keble Munn noted in an interview with *The Guardian* that "We've got all kinds of assurances from the United States government that they are not involved in destabilization, and we would like to be in a position to take them at face value." However, "everyone knows what happened in Chile, although no one could prove who was behind it until afterwards, when Watergate came along" (Payne, 1988, p. 51).

Between 1976 and 1980 the campaign against the Manley regime took on many different forms ranging widely over a variety of incidents indicating that a number of agencies were involved, but with each "not necessarily knowing in detail what the other is up to" (Payne, 1988, p. 53). The bauxite companies, namely Reynolds and Alcoa, began the onslaught by seeking relief through their congressional allies. Senator Orin Hatch, working on behalf of these companies, sought to have aid to Jamaica decreased with the expressed aim of putting pressure on the Manley government (Stephens and Stephens, 1986, p. 127). This action started a series of actions leading to a severe deterioration of Jamaica's balance of payments and negative growth in real GDP (see tables 4.2, 4.3, 4.4). Several factors led to the growing balance of payments deficit. Stephens and Stephens noted the shortfall in receipts from tourism as well as the increase in net investment income payments abroad. Also contributing to this problem was the decrease in the value of bauxite exports. For example, the value of 1975 exports were below that of 1974 up to the end of 1976 (Stephens and Stephens, 1986, p. 128).

The situation for Jamaica, however, was to decline further. Tourist arrivals from the U.S. declined sharply as a result of an adverse campaign in the American media concerning violence in Jamaica. Most of these stories were outright fabrications which bore no relation to the truth. Things became even worse in 1976 when for no apparent reason, a series of violent incidents occurred. The nature of these incidents and the way in which they occurred gave credence to the destabilization charges. They were not traditional political gang violence but rather violence of a callous and destructive nature without an apparent motive (Stephens and Stephens, 1986, p. 132). Coupled with this turn of events, political gang warfare took on a new and ominous intensity. Strange and very destructive fires broke out in many parts of Kingston. The U.S. consulate was mysteriously attacked on several occasions. In one such incident two policemen guarding the Consulate were shot, one fatally. This was followed by what appears to be the random shooting of policemen resulting in a strong protest and a threat to withhold services by the police federation.

As the months went by the violence increased in intensity and destructiveness. In an analysis of the destabilization charges, Stephens and Stephens noted that "In May (1976) armed men set fire to a block of tenement buildings on Orange Street in Kingston, kept the residents from leaving the burning buildings and attacked the police and fire-fighters who were trying to reach the scene. In this attack ten people lost their lives and some 500 their shelter and belongings." They further noted, as have other analysts, that the *Daily Gleaner* (Jamaica's largest and most influential newspaper) reported several days after the incident that "Partisan gang warfare seems to be an unlikely explanation for this event, since an examination of the 1974 returns to the appropriate polling stations showed that the residents had voted in virtually equal numbers for the two parties" (Stephens and Stephens, P. 1986, p. 132).

TABLE 4.2 Rate of Growth of Gross Domestic Product by Industrial Sector at Constant Prices (%)

Industrial sector	1970	1971	1972	1973	1974	1975	1976	1977	1978	1979	1980	1981	1982
Agriculture, forestry and fishing	5.9	11.8	1.8	-8.5	4.3	1.8	1.1	3.0	9.7	-9.8	-6.2	3.9	-6.7
Mining and quarrying	29.1	6.9	6.4	14.3	8.5	-20.2	-20.6	17.5	2.5	-1.6	9.9	1.3	-29.0
Manufacture	6.1	2.3	11.7	0.7	-3.5	2.4	-4.9	-11.6	-5.4	-4.1	-9.7	1.3	4.2
Electricity and water	7.9	12.8	13.5	5.6	0.0	4.1	2.7	-1.6	1.3	-1.7	1.4	1.2	0.0
Construction and installation	20.9	0.5	-2.9	-11.7	-5.4	1.3	-20.0	-20.8	3.6	-0.6	-28.5	1.6	12.9
Distributive trade (wholesale and retail)	5.6	2.8	17.0	-3.8	-16.6	2.8	-18.4	-7.9	-1.4	-4.1	-7.0	5.4	5.8
Transport, storage and communication	11.4	6.0	6.1	1.4	10.2	4.1	-3.4	-5.6	-0.5	0.4	-4.2	0.9	4.1
Financing and insurance services	6.4	-1.1	10.9	6.4	2.0	1.3	-2.6	6.4	-0.1	-7.1	8.6	9.9	-8.0
Real estate and business services	12.8	-1.5	3.5	5.7	-2.1	3.6	0.5	1.8	-2.9	2.7	-0.3	3.4	4.9
Producers of government services	19.5	0.9	14.0	21.1	0.2	5.5	15.9	6.8	4.8	4.8	-0.5	3.1	0.4
Miscellaneous services	12.9	4.5	14.1	-0.4	-5.0	-6.2	-3.0	-3.4	-0.4	-5.7	-5.2	1.1	8.0
Household and private non-profit institutions	26.2	3.9	14.1	20.7	-4.8	-21.9	-13.3	5.3	-19.8	-12.6	-4.0	3.6	8.6
Total Gross Domestic Product at constant prices	12.0	3.0	2.3	1.2	-3.9	-0.4	-6.3	-2.4	0.3	-1.4	-5.3	3.3	0.2

SOURCE Department of Statistics (1981; 1983).

TABLE 4.3 Employment and Unemployment 1972-82 (in 1000 and %)

Date	Total labor force ('000)	Employed labor force ('000)	Unemployed labor force ('000)	Unemployment rate (%)
April 1972	783	598	185	23.6
October 1972	809	624	185	22.8
April 1973	811	637	173	21.4
October 1973	801	621	180	22.4
April 1974	820	642	178	21.8
October 1974	815	648	167	20.4
April 1975	849	677	172	20.3
October 1975	869	685	184	21.2
April 1976	872	693	179	20.5
October 1976	896	679	216	24.2
April 1977	902	680	222	24.6
October 1977	918	699	219	23.8
April 1978	929	715	214	23.0
October 1978	949	702	247	26.0
April 1979	945	715	230	24.4
October 1979	963	663	299	31.1
April 1980	975	703	272	27.9
November 1980	1007	737	270	26.8
April 1981	1007	743	264	26.2
October 1981	1023	761	262	25.6
April 1982	1037	757	281	27.0
October 1982	1049	756	292	27.9

SOURCE NPA (various years).

TABLE 4.4 Exports of Select Goods, 1970-80 (current U.S. $ millions, f.o.b., and %)

Product	1970	1971	1972	1973	1974	1975	1976	1977	1978	1979	1980
Banana	14.2	15.3	14.8	18.3	12.6	16.1	13.2	13.9	17.3	18.2	10.4
Sugar	35.3	39.1	42.1	39.6	81.8	153.8	61.4	63.4	59.5	56.9	54.4
Bauxite	91.0	98.0	86.2	89.4	104.6	149.6	187.5	205.3	234.0	213.5	197.5
Alumina	127.6	136.9	151.1	165.9	297.8	324.8	237.6	323.2	348.3	368.2	534.7
(A) Sub-total	268.1	289.3	294.2	313.2	496.8	644.3	499.7	605.8	659.1	656.8	797.0
(B) Total exports	342.1	370.9	373.7	399.4	605.1	760.0	630.1	724.0	792.1	814.7	965.5
(A)/(B) %	78.4	78.0	78.7	78.4	82.1	84.8	79.3	83.7	83.2	80.6	82.5

SOURCE Bank of Jamaica and Department of Statistics, cited in: IBRD (1982: Statistical Appendix, Table 3.2).

Further an official inquiry into the reasons and perpetrators of the incident conducted by the Chief Justice of Jamaica found no links to either of the two political parties (*Daily Gleaner* February 17, 1977).

This new form of violence and callous disregard for human life had no relationship to the prevailing pattern of partisan political violence in Jamaica. For instance the Peruvian Ambassador was mysteriously shot and killed at his home in Kingston and no trace of the person or persons responsible was ever found. Other incidents which indicated "that forces were at work capable of carefully planning coordinated destructive acts" included the spreading of thick layers of oil on steep and dangerous sections of roads in the Montego Bay area at the time a PNP campaign rally was scheduled (Stephens and Stephens, 1986, p. 132). Members of the security forces, especially the police, were singled out for direct attack. Several policemen were shot while on duty. Likewise, a number of police stations were shot at repeatedly with high powered weapons. In response to the situation and a frightening turn of events where members of the police force and military personnel began to physically assault each other, the Commissioner of Police publicly charged that there was a calculated and deliberate plot to demoralize and undermine the authority of the police force (*Daily Gleaner*, May 28, 1976). This was followed later by a statement from the Minister of National Security, Keble Munn, to the effect that the security forces had in their possession information regarding a specific plan to divide the police and military (Daily Gleaner, November 21, 1976).

Unexplained violence continued to escalate in Jamaica forcing the government finally to declare a state of emergency. There was widespread support for the state of emergency declaration with the notable exception of the JLP whose leader took the position that the existing Suppression of Crimes Act as well as the powers of arrest and detention were sufficient to deal with the situation. Manley argued that the State of Emergency became necessary due to the "recent wanton and ruthless activities" which had "the effect of not only creating fear throughout the country" but were also "slowly bringing the economy to a halt" (*Daily News*, June 20, 1976). As mentioned earlier, the PNP government firmly believed that the violent events of 1976 were part of a U.S. plan to destabilize Jamaica. Manley himself has argued that the CIA was active in Jamaica and was acting through its own agents to destabilize Jamaica. He further noted that heads of the security forces, police, military, and special branch (intelligence) all concurred that the CIA was actively behind the events (Manley, 1982, p. 140).

Having discussed the issue of destabilization and described some of the events attributed to that undertaking, one confronts the question of whether there is evidence to substantiate Manley's claims. The basic problem in answering that question, as Payne argues, is that "what one might call the case for the prosecution..., ranges loosely over a variety of types of evidence and in so doing cannot but identify several different agents of destabilization" (Payne, 1988, p. 53). It is therefore necessary to undertake a very brief examination of the behavior of some of the alleged participants. The most obvious suspects as the instigators of destabilization are the bauxite companies and the U.S. government. There can be no question that the U.S. government played a major role in exerting economic pressure on Jamaica because of the bauxite levy. The U.S. Treasury Department led the way by arguing the case for the discontinuation of any new official loans to Jamaica. The Nixon administration refused to authorize any new official loans and one small loan already authorized was stopped. The Treasury Department accordingly argued against any new capital assistance and would not sanction additional OPIC insurance to Jamaica (O'Flaherty, 1978, p. 154).

U. S. pressure on Jamaica became even more severe once the Jamaican government had begun to establish closer diplomatic links with Cuba. As previously observed, Jamaica's open support for Cuban troop involvement in Angola resulted in a U.S. economic aid embargo. The economic aid embargo lasted until the end of the Ford administration and had a devastating effect on Jamaica's economy throughout 1976. The advent of the Carter administration in the early months of 1977 saw a slight change in U.S. policy resulting in the resumption of some economic aid. By 1980, however, the Jamaican economy had been extensively devastated, due in part to the combined activities of a number of agencies. One agency, the CIA, although an integral part of the U.S. government must be discussed in a different context in view of its traditional clandestine activities. The CIA was accused by Philip Agee, a former employee, as having undertaken acts of destabilization in Jamaica. Agee also named several members of the U.S. embassy staff in Kingston as employees of the CIA, some of whom promptly left the island, in what was seen by many Jamaicans and others in the international community as "a tacit admission of guilt" (Payne, 1988, p. 55). Agee's accusations were further detailed in the December 1977 issue of *Penthouse* magazine in which he charged that Secretary of State Kissinger had agreed to the CIA's covert actions against the Manley regime. The U.S. magazine, *Counterspy*, subsequently published a detailed description of these activities.

The U. S. press also played a significant role in the CIA's efforts against

Jamaica. A number of articles aimed at undermining the reputation of the Manley government were inspired by the CIA as part of its disinformation campaign. Beginning with an article by James Reston in the *New York Times*, a series of other articles were to follow in the *Washington Post, Time, Newsweek* and the *Christian Science Monitor*. Many of these articles, while not only factually inaccurate, conveyed the impression that the Cuban military had taken over Jamaica. The overall effect of the press coverage of the tourist industry was crippling and the industry was not to experience a recovery until the defeat of Manley and the PNP in the 1980 general election. Finally, the Jamaican opposition must be seen as having played a significant role in the destabilization process. The JLP, local businessmen as well as the leading newspaper the *Daily Gleaner*, all contributed to the pressures applied to the Manley regime. The JLP for its part used the "Communist Boogie Man" scare tactic charging that socialism was only a cover for the Communist one party state the PNP government wished to establish. Local businessmen refused to invest while the *Daily Gleaner* printed much of the press coverage coming from the U.S. as well as adding some of its own.

It appears, then, that at least in some areas the charges of deliberate destabilization are supported by the evidence. In other areas, as in the case of the CIA, the charges cannot be proven, at least until the U.S. admits its behavior. Given the nature of covert activities, unless there are congressional hearings similar to those which investigated the Chilean operation, the chances of official U.S. acknowledgement of covert CIA operations in Jamaica are virtually nil. However, "the circumstantial evidence that U.S. agents were active in Jamaica in 1976 is strong—too strong, finally, to be ignored" (Payne, 1988, p. 58). Can it be argued then, that a concerted and deliberate campaign instigated from outside and designed to undermine the Manley government was in fact undertaken by the above named entities? In the years 1974 through 1980 Jamaica's social, political and economic life was in fact thrown off track to the point that when the 1980 general election was held Jamaica was bankrupt, demoralized and in a state of near anarchy.

Notes

1. See Carl Stone, *Class, State, and Democracy in Jamaica: Praeger Special Studies*, New York, London 1986.

2. See *Islands of the Commonwealth Caribbean a Regional Study*, Area Handbook Series, Ed. Meditz, S.W., 1987.

3. See Stone, *Class, State, and Democracy in Jamaica*, 1986; and also John D. Forbes, *Jamaica: Managing Political and Economic Change*, American Enterprise Institute, Washington and London, 1985.

4. See 'Richard Hart Talks about his Experiences in Jamaican Politics', *Jamaica Daily News*, June 8, 1975.

5. *Jamaica Daily News*, September 16, 1974.

6. *Democratic Socialism: The Jamaican Model*, Political Education Committee of the People's National Party, 1974.

7. Ibid

8. For an analysis of the restructuring of the Jamaican economy and a precise definition of the term "Commanding Heights" of the economy see Manley 1974.

9. For an analysis of Democratic Socialism and the DependencyTheory as it affected Jamaica, see Evelyn Huber Stephens and John D. Stephens, *Democratic Socialism in Jamaica: The Political Movement and Social Transofrmation in Dependent Capitalism*. Princeton University Press, Princeton, New Jersey, 1986. See also *Jamaica's Democratic Socialist Experience*, by the same authors, Washington D.C. 1985.

10. National Planning Agency, *Economic and Social Survey: Jamaica 1979* (Kingston, 1980)

11. For an analysis of the economic crisis of the period see Claremont Kirton, "A Preliminary Analysis ofImperialist Penetration and Control via the Foreign Debt: A Study of Jamaica" in Karl Stone and Aggrey Brown (eds). *Essays on Power and Change in Jamaica* (Kingston, 1977), pp. 80-81.

12. National Planning Agency, *Economic and Social Survey: Jamaica 1976* (Kingston, 1977).

13. Sherry Keith and Robert Girling, "Caribbean Conflict: Jamaica and the U.S." *NACLA Report on the Americas*, XII (1978), P. 21.

14. Ibid, p. 24.

15. John D. Forbes, *Jamaica: Managing Political and Economic Change*, 1985, p. 24.

16. For a detailed list of evidence of destabilization in Jamaica see Manley, *Jamaica: Struggle in the Periphery*, pp. 225-9, 1982. See also Payne's summary in *Politics in Jamaica*, 1988, pp. 51-52.

17. Ibid

5
The Caribbean Basin Initiative: Genesis of the Policy

For Jamaica the political and economically turbulent years 1974 through 1980 ended with the defeat of Michael Manley and the PNP government in November 1980. The general election that terminated Manley's rule brought into being a new administration of the Jamaica Labour Party (JLP) led by Edward Seaga. To many observers (Payne, 1988; Stone, 1989; Stephens, E. and Stephens, J. 1985; Ambursley 1983) who studied the passing era, the demise of the Manley regime brought home forcefully to Jamaicans the grim reality that the nation's economic and social infrastructure had eroded to the point where the country could easily have been classified as bankrupt and in a state of near social and political anarchy. Economically, many senior career government officials believed that the nation could not have survived another month.

Into this turmoil came Edward Seaga, the new Prime Minister. Two years earlier he had begun a careful and well implemented media campaign designed to create the image of an astute political and financial genius capable of taking on the task of rectifying Jamaica's multiple economic problems. Indeed to most Jamaicans, even those who may have entertained some doubts, Seaga appeared to be the one political leader who could impose at least some sense of economic and fiscal order on the chaos that resulted from the Manley era. Seaga and the JLP had in their capacity as loyal opposition relentlessly emphasized the idea that the PNP under Michael Manley was a "communist-influenced" party incapable of managing the nation's economy and was responsible for destroying the country's economic base. As events were later to prove, some aspects of the image created by Seaga regarding his fiscal and management skills were not in all cases merely the creation of campaign image makers. In fact, by the time he assumed office he had formulated a number of policy objectives aimed at rebuilding the Jamaican economy. Foremost among these was a U.S. sponsored "rescue programme" for the Caribbean Basin region similar to the Marshall Plan that rebuilt Europe after WWII.

Seaga's plan for rebuilding the economies of the Caribbean Basin countries centered primarily on the concept of a joint development policy that would utilize U.S. and Canadian capital and technological skills coupled with indigenous capital and labor (which is abundantly cheap and plentiful) in the participating countries. The plan further called for the opening of markets in the United States to the products accruing from the joint development projects. Basically, the governments of the United States and Canada would be urged to encourage entrepreneurs in their respective countries to work with their counterparts in the Basin Countries in researching and identifying projects suitable for development. These projects would include traditional exports such as sugar, bananas, apparel, leather goods, exotic liquors, textiles, and tourism. The plan also included the introduction of non-traditional industries including electronics, chemicals, and "screw-driver" assembly manufacturing.

The slogan Seaga used to explain this concept was "Trade and Aid," meaning the United States and Canada should assist these countries to build a viable manufacturing and export base which would in turn help to develop their economies. This would prevent the establishment of permanent dependence on grants and other forms of aid from the United States and Canada. Confidential interviews with senior party and government officials in Jamaica suggested that Seaga first discussed his ideas with the heads of government of a number of the English speaking countries in the Caribbean. The idea reportedly was well received, especially in view of the fact that such a plan if successful would help to establish a more comprehensive form of economic as well poliical independence. Conceivably it would also help the countries in the region which since 1974 were seriously affected by the escalating cost of oil and declining prices for their major exports (bauxite, sugar, and coffee). (See Tables 5.1 and 5.2)

Very little evidence exists to determine the extent to which Seaga in the early stages of strategic economic planning, discussed his ideas with key members of the JLP. He did, however, on a number of occasions during the 1980 election campaign suggest that the United States initiate a "Marshall Plan" for the Caribbean area. In view of such public pronouncements it is safe to assume that at a minimum the Minister of Foreign Affairs, Hugh Shearer, as well as other members of Seaga's "inner-cabinet" must have been aware of the idea at an early date. Seaga had also on many other occasions expressed a concern for the economic crisis in the area which was amplified by the deep rooted structural problems. The seriousness of the crisis is reflected in such

TABLE 5.1 Gross Domestic Product by Industrial Sector in Purchaser's Values at Constant Prices ($ millions)

Industrial sector	1970	1971	1972	1973	1974	1975	1976	1977	1978	1979	1980	1981	1982
Agriculture, forestry and fishing	149.8	167.5	170.6	146.9	153.2	156.0	157.6	162.3	178.0	160.6	150.6	156.4	145.9
Mining and quarrying	139.7	149.3	158.9	181.6	197.0	157.2	124.9	146.7	150.4	148.0	162.7	164.8	117.0
Manufacture	348.1	356.1	397.8	401.1	387.2	396.5	377.2	350.6	331.9	318.3	287.5	291.1	303.2
Electricity and water	16.4	18.5	21.0	22.2	22.2	23.1	23.7	23.4	23.7	23.3	23.6	23.9	23.9
Construction and installation	261.7	263.1	255.5	225.7	213.5	210.8	168.6	133.6	138.3	137.4	98.3	99.9	112.7
Distributive trade (wholesale and retail)	423.2	435.2	509.4	481.9	401.7	413.0	337.0	310.5	306.3	293.7	273.1	287.8	304.4
Transport, storage and communication	109.1	115.6	122.6	124.3	137.0	142.6	137.7	130.0	129.4	129.9	124.5	125.6	130.8
Financing and insurance services	78.6	77.7	86.0	91.6	93.4	94.6	92.1	98.0	97.8	90.9	98.7	108.4	99.8
Real estate and business services	194.1	191.1	197.8	208.9	204.6	211.9	212.9	216.7	210.4	216.0	215.4	222.6	233.6
Producers of government services	180.1	181.7	207.2	250.9	251.4	265.1	307.3	328.3	344.1	360.5	358.5	369.5	370.9
Miscellaneous services	106.1	110.9	126.5	125.9	119.6	112.2	108.8	105.0	105.5	98.6	93.5	94.5	102.1
Household and private non-profit institutions	27.9	29.0	33.1	39.9	38.0	29.7	25.7	27.1	21.7	19.0	18.2	18.9	20.5
Less imputed service charges	52.6	53.5	55.1	60.3	65.7	68.9	64.0	70.4	68.0	55.0	67.1	65.8	64.0
Total Gross Domestic Product at Constant Prices	1982.2	2042.2	2231.3	2240.6	2153.1	2143.8	2009.5	1961.8	1968.5	1941.2	1837.5	1897.7	1900.9

SOURCE Department of Statistics, (1981; 1983).

TABLE 5.2 Rate of Growth of Gross Domestic Product by Industrial Sector at Constant Prices (%)

Industrial sector	1970	1971	1972	1973	1974	1975	1976	1977	1978	1979	1980	1981	1982
Agriculture, forestry and fishing	5.9	11.8	1.8	-8.5	4.3	1.8	1.1	3.0	9.7	-9.8	-6.2	3.9	-6.7
Mining and quarrying	29.1	6.9	6.4	14.3	8.5	-20.2	-20.6	17.5	2.5	-1.6	9.9	1.3	-29.0
Manufacture	6.1	2.3	11.7	0.7	-3.5	2.4	-4.9	-11.6	-5.4	-4.1	-9.7	1.3	4.2
Electricity and water	7.9	12.8	13.5	5.6	0.0	4.1	2.7	-1.6	1.3	-1.7	1.4	1.2	0.0
Construction and installation	20.9	0.5	-2.9	-11.7	-5.4	1.3	-20.0	-20.8	3.6	-0.6	-28.5	1.6	12.9
Distributive trade (wholesale and retail)	5.6	2.8	17.0	-3.8	-16.6	2.8	-18.4	-7.9	-1.4	-4.1	-7.0	5.4	5.8
Transport, storage and communication	11.4	6.0	6.1	1.4	10.2	4.1	-3.4	-5.6	-0.5	0.4	-4.2	0.9	4.1
Financing and insurance services	6.4	-1.1	10.9	6.4	2.0	1.3	-2.6	6.4	-0.1	-7.1	8.6	9.9	-8.0
Real estate and business services	12.8	-1.5	3.5	5.7	-2.1	3.6	0.5	1.8	-2.9	2.7	-0.3	3.4	4.9
Producers of government services	19.5	0.9	14.0	21.1	0.2	5.5	15.9	6.8	4.8	4.8	-0.5	3.1	0.4
Miscellaneous services	12.9	4.5	14.1	-0.4	-5.0	-6.2	-3.0	-3.4	-0.4	-5.7	-5.2	1.1	8.0
Household and private non-profit institutions	26.2	3.9	14.1	20.7	-4.8	-21.9	-13.3	5.3	-19.8	-12.6	-4.0	3.6	8.6
Total Gross Domestic Product at constant prices	12.0	3.0	2.3	1.2	-3.9	-0.4	-6.3	-2.4	0.3	-1.4	-5.3	3.3	0.2

SOURCE Department of Statistics (1981; 1983).

indicators as inflation, unemployment, a declining gross domestic product (GDP), and an ever worsening balance of payments. (See Tables 5.3, 5.4 and 5.5)

Recognizing the urgency of the situation and the need for quick decisive action, Seaga first publicly outlined his plan for rebuilding the economies of the Caribbean Basin countries in a speech in Washington, D.C. in which he called on the United States and its allies to underwrite the cost of what was first conceived as a "Mini-Marshall Plan". It is believed that a rough outline of the plan was discussed with President-elect Reagan and members of his staff on a visit to Washington by Seaga prior to Reagan's inauguration. Members of the Reagan team who would have been well acquainted with the details of Seaga's plan included Secretary of State Alexander Haig, White House Chief of Staff James Baker, and Deputy Chief of Staff Michael Deaver. What transpired in the Reagan White House, in terms of strategy planning after Seaga's introduction of his plan, is not clear. What is clear, however, is that Reagan and his staff saw, at least in the early stages, some merit in Seaga's ideas and proceeded to develop a policy from which the plan would be implemented.

Seaga's plan was further discussed at a conference held in the Bahamas in July 1981. At that time U.S. Secretary of State Haig along with the Foreign Ministers of Venezuela, Canada, and Mexico arrived at an agreement adopting a joint approach for providing development aid in the Caribbean Basin.[1] The policy was thereafter presented publicly as the "Caribbean Basin Initiative" in a speech by President Reagan to the Organization of American States on February 24, 1982 (*Congressional Quarterly*, Feb. 27, 1982, pp. 491-493). A legislative bill which sets forth the economic aspects of the program entitled the Caribbean Basin Economic Recovery Act was submitted as a formal proposal to Congress on March 17 and introduced March 18, 1982 as HR 5900 and S2237 (*Congressional Quarterly*, March 27, 1982). The act became law on August 5, 1983 and the duty-free entry provisions went into effect January 1, 1984.[2]

The Caribbean Basin Initiative

The Caribbean Basin Initiative (CBI), as originally conceived by Seaga, was to be a broad program aimed at promoting economic development primarily through joint public and private sector initiatives in the countries of Central America and the Caribbean. The basic goal of the CBI was the expansion of foreign and domestic investments in non-traditional sectors. It would employ

TABLE 5.3 Balance-of-Payments Summary, 1969-82 (U.S. $ Millions, current)

	1969	1970	1971	1972	1973	1974	1975	1976	1977	1978	1979	1980	1981	1982
Current account balance	−123.6	−152.6	−174.8	−125.3	−180.7	−167.0	−282.7	−302.7	−68.2	−86.7	−142.6	−166.3	−336.8	−426.4
Capital movement (net)	118.2	160.9	195.7	74.6	137.1	243.2	208.9	48.3	101.5	9.8	−10.4	105.1	247.2	508.2
Government external borrowing	12.4	−1.4	4.9	23.2	36.7	90.1	124.2	79.2	38.6	178.9	71.2	226.6	240.2	469.1
Identified private capital	105.8	162.3	190.8	51.4	100.4	153.1	84.7	−30.9	62.9	−169.1	−81.6	−121.5	7.0	39.1
Allocation of SDRs	–	6.3	5.7	5.9	–	–	–	–	–	–	10.0	10.0	10.0	–
Net errors and omissions	−8.2	6.5	17.8	−9.6	13.1	−16.7	−7.2	−7.5	−34.9	−0.6	2.1	1.0	−10.9	n.a.
Overall surplus/deficit (increase = −)	13.6	−21.1	−44.4	54.4	30.5	−59.5	81.0	261.9	14.6	77.5	140.9	50.2	90.5	−81.8

SOURCE Except for 1977 and 1982, all data from Bank of Jamaica. 1969 cited in Girvan et al. (1980): Table 7). 1969-76 converted to US$ using IFS conversion rate. 1977 data from IDB (1982: Table 40). 1982 data from NPA (various years).

TABLE 5.4 Share of Exports to Major Trading Partners, 1970-80

	1970	1971	1972	1973	1974	1975	1976	1977	1978	1979	1980
United States	51.9	45.0	42.4	41.2	47.1	40.3	48.0	47.4	43.2	44.9	37.1
United Kingdom	15.6	19.6	21.7	22.8	16.8	22.3	15.7	18.5	22.2	19.1	19.3
Caricom countries	3.1	4.8	5.8	6.3	5.3	4.5	6.9	6.7	7.3	7.6	5.9
Canada	8.2	8.3	7.1	5.5	5.6	3.3	5.0	8.0	7.7	6.0	3.9
Norway	7.9	8.7	11.5	10.4	11.5	9.5	10.1	9.5	6.4	5.1	10.8
Latin America	1.1	1.1	0.9	1.4	1.8	1.0	3.5	1.9	2.8	2.7	1.6
EEC countries	1.3	0.7	0.9	3.2	1.1	0.6	1.6	1.1	1.2	1.0	0.9
Other	10.9	11.8	9.8	9.2	10.8	18.4	9.2	6.9	9.2	13.7	20.6
Total Jamaica	100.0	100.0	100.0	100.0	100.0	100.0	100.0	100.0	100.0	100.0	100.0

NOTE Figures may not all add up to 100% because of rounding.
SOURCE Bank of Jamaica and Department of Statistics. As from: IBRD (1982: Statistical Appendix).

TABLE 5.4A Share of Imports from Major Trading Partners, 1970-80

	1970	1971	1972	1973	1974	1975	1976	1977	1978	1979	1980
United States	43.0	39.6	37.2	37.9	35.2	37.4	37.2	36.0	36.8	31.8	31.4
Latin America	6.0	6.6	7.0	9.4	17.6	16.1	16.4	18.3	18.5	19.3	17.0
United Kingdom	19.1	19.8	19.2	16.4	12.4	13.1	10.9	9.7	10.4	9.8	6.7
EEC countries	8.1	9.1	8.7	9.8	8.3	6.8	6.3	5.9	6.1	6.7	4.6
Caricom countries	1.7	2.4	5.3	5.2	7.6	8.4	7.0	5.7	5.5	5.7	7.2
Canada	9.0	7.5	7.2	6.7	5.4	4.9	5.9	5.6	5.6	4.9	6.0
Other	13.1	15.0	14.6	14.5	13.5	13.3	16.4	18.8	17.1	21.9	27.0
Total Jamaica	100.0	100.0	100.0	100.0	100.0	100.0	100.0	100.0	100.0	100.0	100.0

NOTE Figures may not all add up to 100% because of rounding.
SOURCE Bank of Jamaica and Department of Statistics. As from: IBRD (1982: Statistical Appendix).

TABLE 5.5 Rate of Growth of Gross Domestic Product by Industrial Sectors at Constant Prices (%)

Industrial Sector	1974	1975	1976	1977	1978
Agriculture, Forestry and Fishing	2.0	1.4	-4.1	7.9	9.3
Mining and Quarrying	13.5	-23.5	-19.0	17.8	2.0
Manufacture	-3.5	2.4	-5.1	-9.6	-4.8
Electricity and Water	.1	4.1	2.7	-1.6	1.3
Construction and Installation	-5.0	-.8	-20.3	-23.4	2.8
Distributive Trade (Wholesale and Retail)	-16.7	7.9	-16.7	-7.5	-11.7
Transport, Storage and Communication	10.1	3.9	-3.5	-.9	-3.7
Financing and Insurance Services	10.4	7.7	-13.5	3.4	-2.0
Real Estate and Business Services	-2.1	3.6	.5	1.8	-2.4
Producers of Government Services	25.1	-13.1	7.6	9.7	4.1
Miscellaneous Services	-5.0	-6.2	-3.3	-7.0	2.0
Household and Private Non-Profit Institutions	-4.8	-21.9	-8.0	5.9	-17.4
Total Gross Domestic Product at Constant Prices	-0.7	-2.6	-8.3	-2.0	-1.7

foreign and domestic investment capital and the abundant cheap labor of the region. This would be backed up with the guarantee of easy non-encumbered entry of the region's products into the U.S. and Canadian markets. This would help to diversify the economies of the CBI countries while expanding their exports. Simply put, the "marrying" of foreign and domestic capital with readily available cheap labour would be the spark needed to generate economic developmental energy in the region.

In theory the Caribbean Basin Economic Recovery Act (CBERA) of 1982 embodied in basic form some of the principles envisioned by Seaga. The major elements of the CBI program contained in the statute signed into law as the Caribbean Basin Economic Recovery Act (CBERA) required:

a. Duty-free entry to the United States for a period of 12 years commencing January 1, 1984, for a wide range of basic products manufactured in CBI countries primarily as an incentive for investment and expanded export production.[3]

An interesting aspect of this section of the CBI is that products eligible for customs-duty free entry may still be subjected to federal excise taxes. The most notable example in this regard are rum and other liquors, the largest export from the participating countries. In addition, products are still required to comply with all applicable laws, regulations, and standards such as those designed to protect U.S. consumers and industry from unfair trading practices and potentially harmful or unsafe products. However, not all products are eligible for duty-free entry into the United States under the CBI. Indeed the law specifically excludes a number of articles vital to the success of the program (U.S. Dept. of Commerce, 1989 Guidebook the CBI).

b. Increased United States economic assistance to the region designed to aid private sector development through the financing of essential imports, establishment of development banks, Chambers of Commerce, skills training programs, industrial free zones, and other essential infrastructure.
c. A deduction on U.S. taxes for companies that hold their business conventions in qualifying Caribbean Basin countries. This provision was directed at encouraging tourism in the participating countries.
d. Caribbean Basin country self-help efforts aimed at improving the local business community along with support efforts by investors and exporters.
e. Involvement of a wide range of U.S. Government, state government, and private sector promotion programs in trade and investment financing,

business development missions, technical assistance, and what was termed a U.S. Government special access program for textiles and apparel.
f. Support from other trading partners and multinational development institutions primarily the World Bank, the Inter-American Development Bank and the International Monetary Fund (IMF).

The Caribbean Basin Initiative included 24 developing countries of varying sizes located in Central America, the Caribbean, and northern South America. Of the potentially eligible countries in the designated area, Cuba was explicitly excluded, while Nicaragua, the Cayman Islands, the Turks and Caicos Islands, Suriname and Anguilla were classified as "non-designated." In 1988 Panama lost its beneficiary status due to the Noregia government's alleged refusal to cooperate with the United States drug control efforts. (Panama was reinstated to beneficiary status immediately after the U.S. invasion in December 1989). Guyana, one of the countries expected to be included among the original beneficiaries was not accorded that status for a number of years, until a new government adopted a more conservative economic and political posture.[4]

The Caribbean Basin region is of geopolitical importance to the United States. Indeed, the region is often seen as forming the third border of the U.S. It also contains several vital sea lanes through which a large percentage of U.S. oil imports must flow. The region is also an extremely important market for U.S. exports and it is the second largeest source of illegal immigration into the U.S. At the time the initiative was announced President Reagan described the offer of one-way free trade as the centerpiece of his proposal. It is, however, important to note that products from the region were already accorded a fairly non-restrictive entry into the U.S. market. Indeed, some of the existing duties at the time, affected exports to the U.S. of special interest to the countries involved and in some cases limited export expansion in others. The CBI would, in the reasoning of its proponents despite evidence contrary, eliminate most duties on imports to the United States, with textiles, apparel, and sugar subject to special policies such as existing tariff agreements between individual countries and the U.S. government.[5]

In theory then, the Reagan Administration's proposed legislation would seek to use trade and aid to promote political stability as well as economic growth in the Caribbean Basin region. Among other things, the CBI would, as envisioned by the policy-makers, create a one-way free trade zone, where the small nations of the region would have an opportunity for export-led growth through duty free access to the U.S. market. The proposed legislation would also provide $350 million in U.S. economic aid for 1982 to El Salvador in particular and the other Caribbean Islands in general. It also included incentives to expand U.S. foreign investments in the region, as well as some proposals for strengthening the private sector in the Caribbean nations.

President Reagan in his 1982 speech to the OAS pointedly noted that the CBI was needed to strengthen the nations of the Caribbean and Central America and to help bolster them against outside subversion. He observed that those "countries are under economic seige. Economic disaster had drained their money reserves, stimulated illegal immigration to the United States and shaken their political stability." "The CBI," he proclaimed "provided a fresh opening to the enemies of freedom, national independence and peaceful development."[6]

In a revealing indication of the direction he wished and intended for the CBI to go, President Reagan said that the proposal showed that the United States was ready to counter communist activity in the region. "If we do not act promptly and decisively in defense of freedom," he argued, "new Cubas will arise from the ruins of today's conflicts." Reagan also said that the United States would concentrate on the economic problems of the region. It was the intention of his administration to spend as much as five times more than it had previously on economic assistance to the region including the resources allocated for CBI. However, as was revealed in the implementation of the CBI, the Reagan administration instead emphasized military assistance rather than economic.

The Reagan administration, however, did everything in the early stages of the proposal to give the impression that the CBI was a panacea that would solve the region's economic, and by extension, political problems. In their early statements, administration spokesmen placed a great deal of emphasis on the development aspects of the proposal. In February 1982, for example, U.S. Trade Representative William Brock said that the initiative was designed to respond simultaneously with trade and aid to the Caribbean's short and long term needs. In testimony before the Senate Foreign Relations Committee on March 25, Brock noted that the CBI should be able to effectively deal with the basic problems confronting the region.[7]

In similar testimony before the Senate committee, Deputy Secretary of State Walter Stoessel noted that "security, democracy, and economic development are clearly linked together" in the Caribbean area. Stoessel added that the CBI plan was intended to help those small countries survive the present crisis, achieve self sustaining growth, and "give them hope in their futures with Western values as the foundation for their freedom and independence." In the same Senate Hearings, AID Administrator Peter McPherson argued that the CBI was not an aid based development program, as the 1960s Alliance for Progress had been. What the administration had tried to create, he noted, "is a program that is based more on the development of an indigenous private sector—so they can develop the institutional means for preserving political pluralism".[8]

Reactions to the CBI proposal were not in all cases favorable, or received with the same level of enthusiasm exhibited by the Reagan administration. As early as March 23, five days after the proposal was formally submitted to Congress, Representative Jonathan Bingham (D-N.Y.) chairman of the House Foreign Affairs Subcommittee on International Economic Policy and Trade, pointedly warned administration officials that they should not expect rapid congressional action on the entire CBI proposal as presented. Bingham suggested that the economic aid portion of the CBI be included in a separate bill in order that that section move faster, while the rest of the proposals worked their way through congressional committees (*Congressional Quarterly*, March 27, 1982). Indeed from the very inception of the program several elements, comprising the heart of the package, were considered controversial. The foreign trade portions of the plan were opposed by some U.S. business groups and labor unions. They expressed fears that goods manufactured in the Caribbean would undersell those locally produced and that there was a strong possibility that firms located in the US might choose to shift their base of operations to the Caribbean if their products faced no tariff barriers and the same tax credits could be obtained on their investments in both the U.S. and the Caribbean. Farm groups expressed concern that new competition from the Caribbean fruit and winter vegetable growers would adversely affect their business. The U.S. sugar industry mounted strong opposition to the relevant sections of the CBI and expressed concern that it would undermine the U.S. sugar price support system. The same could be said for liquor producers in the Virgin Islands and Puerto Rico, who feared that they might have to close some of their local distilleries if too much rum was imported into the U.S. from Caribbean countries.

On the other hand, many critics in the economic and foreign affairs arena in the United States and the Caribbean region, argued that the Reagan administration's CBI proposal lacked scope and thus was limited in its ability to effectively deal with the real needs of the region. Abraham F. Lowenthal, in one of the earliest constructive critiques of the initiative, noted that:

> The allocations for assistance suggest that obtaining aid from the United States will depend more on a country's attitudes toward Cuba, U.S. foreign policies, and U.S. private investment than on the country's economic need or development prospects. The CBI reflects the administration's interest in military security, political loyalty, and advantages for U.S. firms, rather than U.S. concern for the region's

long-term development.[9]

Critics argued that the small amounts of additional bilateral economic aid in the package would not be able to offset the staggering amounts of outflows of private capital from the region, much less provide any semblance of a net increase in local investments. Liberal Congressional Democrats criticized the plan charging that no provisions were made to provide additional funds for traditional "development" aid programs in health, education and agriculture. Representative Michael Barnes D-MD.) chair of the House Inter-American Affairs Subcommittee, complained that the Reagan administration was "sending conflicting signals" by simultaneously proposing the CBI and seeking to reduce U.S. contributions to the soft-loan window of the Inter-American Development Bank, the agency that provides low-interest loans for development programs in the underdeveloped nations of Latin America (*Congressional Quarterly*, 1982). The critics further argued that the U.S. proposal to reduce the size of the multilateral bank programs in the Latin American area would more than offset any increased aid from this bilateral program.

To help prove their point that the CBI fell far short of the type of program needed, some critics said that possibly only about seven percent by value of the Caribbean's exports to the United States (meaning articles other than sugar, petroleum, textiles, and goods entering free under the regular tariff or GSP rules) would be affected by the elimination of U.S. duties.[10] Doubts were also expressed as to whether sufficient investment would be made available under the CBI to support a major expansion in the region's duty-free exports or any significant transformation of the Caribbean economies. (See Table 5.6)

Finally, some critics also voiced concern that too much of the CBI bilateral aid money was earmarked for short-term balance of payments support and not enough for project aid aimed at overcoming the many obstacles which have hindered growth and development over the past several years. Some critics even insisted that an unusually large amount of the bilateral aid was set aside by the administration specifically for Central America (a total of $243 million out of a total of $350 million). While in fact the economic aid in itself was relatively non-controversial, some members of Congress felt it necessary to state their concern regarding the administration's proposal to increase foreign aid at a time when domestic programs were drastically reduced. Rep. Bill Goodling (R-PA.) a supporter of Reagan's proposals, noted that while the emergency funds allocated for the CBI were small, he found it difficult to explain to his constituents how it was possible for the administration to increase foreign aid.

To the most vociferous critics the CBI appeared to be mainly a vehicle for strengthening U.S. security policy in the Central America/Caribbean area. One of the critics, Representative Mervyn M. Dymally (D-CA) accused the administration of attempting to mislead the Congress by inappropriately labeling

TABLE 5.6 Data on Potential Beneficiaries of the Caribbean Basin Initiative, 1980

Total Area: 494,684 square miles
Total Population: $39 million
Total GDP: $45 billion

Country	Area (square miles)	Population (millions of persons)	Gross Domestic Product ($ millions)	Exports to U.S.[1] ($ millions)	Imports from U.S.[1] (% of total)
Bahamas	5,380	.24	1,267	1,302[2]	11
Barbados	166	.25	815	85	34
Belize	8,866	.16	165	57	44
Cayman Islands	118	.15	—	3	—
Costa Rica	19,700	2.24	4,847	348	34
Dominican Republic	18,712	5.43	6,733	634	44
Eastern Caribbean	812	.65	500	37	45
Anguilla, Antigua and Barbuda, British Virgin Islands, Dominica, Grenada, Montserrat, Saint Christopher-Nevis, Saint Lucia, Saint Vincent and the Grenadines					
El Salvador	8,260	4.50	3,484	404	31
Guatemala	42,000	7.26	7,852	423	35
Guyana	83,000	.79	524	123	28
Haiti	10,714	5.01	1,453	240	57
Honduras	43,277	3.69	2,538	432	41
Jamaica	4,411	2.19	2,402	380	29
Netherlands Antilles	394	.27	—	2,436[2]	6
Nicaragua	147,888	2.70	1,566	206	34
Panama	28,753	1.94	3,511	262	22
Suriname	70,060	.39	109	114	29
Trinidad and Tobago	1,980	1.14	6,708	2,326[2]	26
Turks and Caicos Islands	192	.01	—	3	—

[1]Source: International Monetary Fund, *Directories of Trade Statistics Yearbook*, 1974-80.
[2]Primarily processed products of imported crude oil

the proposal. Speaking on behalf of the Congressional Black Caucus, Dymally told two House Foreign Affairs subcommittees that in his opinion most of the direct aid under the CBI would go to the Spanish-speaking countries of Central America, rather than to the predominantly black island nations in the Caribbean (*Congressional Quarterly*, 1982). Significantly, El Salvador alone was later awarded as much as $128 million.

Predictably the Reagan administration and its allies disputed the accuracy of the critics charges, insisting that the CBI was in fact a sound and rational policy conducive to the future development of the Caribbean. They argued that the foreign policy costs of failing to adopt and aggressively implement the CBI plan would prove to be enormous, particularly in view of the fact that the United States had through repeated policy statements contributed to the rising level of expectations in the area. The advantages to the United States resulting from a strong and vibrant Caribbean economy would, they argued, far outweigh the costs from any small dislocations in segments of the U.S. economy.[11] They argued also that most of the 1983 aid money allocated for Central America was necessary in view of the economic problems in that region. Thus, on a per capita basis, they concluded, the Caribbean islands were getting the larger share in comparison to El Salvador. In this regard they contended the trade sections of the CBI package were really more important in terms of their potential long-term impact on the entire region's development prospects than the allocation pattern for 1983 economic aid.

Special measures designed to benefit U.S. insular possessions, particularly the Virgin Islands and Puerto Rico were included in the CBI provisions. The premise underlying this policy is that these two U.S. flag territories should be accorded extra help to withstand the competition that would result from the CBI. The administration's plan therefore advocated a transfer to the two U.S. possessions of all the Federal Excise Tax collected on imported rum if that product received duty-free status in the Caribbean free trade zone. The plan would also count value added in the form of goods and services from the Virgin Islands and Puerto Rico as Caribbean imports in calculating the 25 percent Caribbean content requirement for duty free entry. The expectation was that Caribbean nations would be encouraged to work closely with firms in the U.S. possessions as they attempted to expand their duty free exports under the plan.[12]

President Reagan sought legislation aimed at reducing the local input requirement for duty free export to the United States from all of the insular possessions from 50% to 30%. The rationale behind this proposed legislation was that inasmuch as the 25% allowance for the CBI would apply to all United States insular possessions, their exporters would have a choice as to which of the local content requirements they wished to follow. Firms in Puerto Rico and the Virgin Islands, as with their counterparts on the U.S. mainland, could also use existing international trade commission safeguards to help protect them from injurious competition. Other provisions announced by the President as part of the CBI program included the use of the administration's existing legal authority to encourage the growth of the private sector in Caribbean nations in other ways, such as working with the respective governments in the region to design development strategies aimed at emphasizing private sector activity. U.S. aid would help to coordinate programs aimed at promoting regional trade, improving transportation, and removing impediments to private sector expansion.

The United States Department of Agriculture (USDA) was slated to play an important role in the CBI, such as providing technical and other forms of assistance in the area of agro-industry. Such a role was considered important in helping Caribbean nations expand their agricultural exports to the U.S. Along with USDA, other U.S. government agencies would engage in programs of their own in an effort to identify and solve problems that could negatively affect the growth of the private sector in the target area. President Reagan noted that the U.S. Export-Import Bank would undertake a program expansion aimed specifically at financing trade in the Caribbean. This was necessary in view of the hesitancy on the part of most private U.S. banks to extend credit to countries in the area. The primary reason given for the withholding of credit was the region's "instability", though the Caribbean region in general and the English speaking Caribbean nations in particular have experienced more stable politics and steady economic growth than most former colonial areas. Thus, credits needed to stimulate and finance further development were unavailable due primarily to the lenders' risk perceptions. To overcome the shortage of credit, estimated to be in excess of $1 billion, the CBI provided for the new role of the Export-Import bank and for the U.S. export finance agency to begin considering the provision of new guarantees for short-term loans to countries included in the initiative.[13]

Congressional Action

Congressional action regarding the implementation of the Administration's CBI plan commenced with the introduction on March 18, 1982 of Bill HR 5900 in the U.S. House of Representatives by the minority leader Robert Michel (R-ILL) and the majority leader Jim Wright (D-Tex). In the U.S. Senate, Bill S 2237 was introduced by the majority leader Robert Dole (R-Kan) and several co-sponsors from both parties. The main elements of the initiative included a $350 million emergency economic aid package for selected nations, the lifting of most of the existing U.S. duties on imports from the region, and tax breaks aimed at encouraging U.S. business interests to invest in the Caribbean Basin Region.

The legislation was referred jointly to the House Committees on Ways and Means and Foreign Affairs and the Senate Committees on Finance, and Foreign Relations. As subsequent events would reveal passage of the CBI bill through Congress was not as easy as originally anticipated. Indeed administration officials expressed concern that the Congress might simply approve some of the economic aid and then shelve the rest of the proposals. This concern was heightened even more by the fact that various parts of the proposal would necessarily have to work their way through six congressional committees; both the House and Senate Appropriations committees, the Finance and Foreign Relations committees in the Senate, and the Foreign Affairs and Ways and Means Committees in the House. The Trade Sub-committee of the House Ways and Means Committee proposed narrowing the free trade provisions of the Administration's plan. In marking up the proposed legislation it adopted an amendment (which had been strongly supported by the U.S. leather products industry) excluding from the duty-free provisions of the bill footwear, luggage, and other mostly leather goods which were not duty-free under the General System of Preferences (GSP).

In what was one of the most damaging actions undertaken during the legislative process, the Trade Sub-committee established specific quotas on the duty-free entry of rum produced in the CBI region. It also tightened the provisions in the bill allowing Caribbean exports to contain only 25 percent regional value added. This was accomplished by adding a number of guidelines which defined in greater detail the eligibility standards under that rule. Finally, the subcommittee incorporated into the bill the change President Reagan had sought lowering the local content threshold from fifty to thirty percent for duty free imports from U.S. insular possessions. The CBI legislation remained stuck in the Ways and Means Committee following the Trade Subcommittee's action, due in part to the level and intensity of criticism directed at the plan by various domestic groups who saw the package as detrimental to their interests. It quickly became apparent that several elements of the CBI package were highly controversial. Notably the fact that elimination of U.S. duties would not occur automatically for every country in the region. The bill specifically prohibited the extension of the free-trade provisions to four categories of countries: those classified as communist; those that have nationalized or seized property owned by U.S. citizens; countries categorized as having not acted in "good faith" to recognize binding arbitration awards in favor of U.S. companies or citizens; and countries that give preferential treatment to the products of developed countries other than the U.S. These provisions prompted Rep. Michael Barnes, (D-MD.) to charge that the restrictions were written to enable the Reagan Administration "to reward our friends" (*Congressional Quarterly* March 1982). As earlier noted, a number of labor unions and business groups registered opposition to the foreign trade sections of the initiative.

Moreover, opposition to the CBI did not arise from groups expressing self interest only. From other perspectives several economic and foreign affairs observers (Lowenthal, 1982; Newfarmer, 1982; Fienberg, 1982; Watson, 1985) commented that the initiative was simply too confining in its scope to ever begin to address the overwhelming needs of the Caribbean. Many (Fienberg, 1982; Newfarmer, 1982) took the position that the additional bilateral economic aid provisions in the package were too small to offset the huge outflows of private capital from the region, let along provide any net increase in local investments. In addition, it was argued, the U.S. proposal for reducing the size of the multilateral bank programs in the Latin American area more than offset any increased aid from this bilateral program. Finally, many critics (Sanford, 1982; Payne, 1988; Pastor, 1982) also expressed concern that too much of the CBI bilateral aid money was allocated for short-term balance of payments support and very little was intended for project aid geared at helping to overcome those obstacles that have seriously hampered growth and socioeconomic development in the past.[14]

Eventually on November 30, 1982, in preparation for a trip to four Latin American countries, President Reagan met with several members of Congress in an attempt to explain "the importance" of the CBI proposal. This meeting resulted in an apparent agreement with Dan Rostenkowski, Chairman of the House, Ways and Means Committee regarding passage of the trade portion of the CBI plan.[15] The full committee on Ways and Means marked up and reported its version of the CBI legislation by a 28-6 vote on December 11, 1982. This bill included most of the provisions approved earlier by the Trade Subcommittee, significantly, the full committee approved a number of changes in the draft submitted by the subcommittee. According to Sanford: "First, it dropped the proposed quotas and limits on imports of rum from CBI nations. Second, it excluded petroleum and petroleum products from duty free treatment. Third, it required the CBI beneficiaries to take action so that expanding their agricultural exports to the U.S. does not adversely affect their local food production for consumption by poor people."[16]

In addition the Ways and Means Committee deleted the investment tax credit and accelerated depreciation provisions proposed by the Administration in its original bill. Title II of the final committee bill did, however, include some tax provisions. As noted by Sanford, "It stipulated: (a) that the excise tax revenues from future rum imports from the CBI region would be transferred to Puerto Rico and the Virgin Islands; (b) that the cost of attending certain kinds of conventions in the Caribbean will be deductible as if the convention were held in the United States, providing the Caribbean host country has entered into an exchange-of-information agreement on tax matters with the treasury."[17] A number of amendments aimed at granting certain industries and certain products protection from the duty-free provisions of the bill were defeated by the Ways and Means Committee, such as a motion to retain the quotas and limits on imported rum. Finally, it rejected a motion to extend accelerated cost recovery tax benefits to investments in Puerto Rico and the Virgin Islands.

The U.S. House of Representatives approved the Ways and Means Committee's proposed legislation on December 17, 1982 by a 260-142 recorded vote. In the course of its deliberations, the House voted to keep the existing tariff protection for canned tuna and to exclude that product from duty free treatment under the bill, but it rejected a similar proposal aimed at excluding imports of tobacco products. As a final act the House rejected (172-226) an amendment designed to establish quotas and ceilings on the duty free importation of Caribbean rum.[18]

Both House and Senate foreign affairs panels ended up making significant changes to the CBI plan during their respective consideration of the proposed legislation. For its part the House Foreign Affairs Committee made substantial revisions to the foreign aid portion of the CBI bill when it reported title II of the legislation on July 15, 1983. In essence the committee sought to have more emphasis placed on long-term development and less on short-term balance of payments support in the program. In doing so it used HR 6755, an alternative bill introduced during the debates as its point of departure in amending the Administration's proposed plan. This bill incorporated most of the changes that were earlier recommended by the committee's International Economic Policy and Inter-American Affairs subcommittees. The two subcommittees had on May 11, voted to place limits on the amount any one country could receive under the CBI aid program, thereby reducing the amount set aside for El Salvador, as well as requiring that most of the CBI money be used for development rather than balance of payment support. The issue of financial and military aid to El Salvador presented one of the greatest threats to the passage of the CBI Bill. Recognizing the possibility of the Reagan administration using the CBI proposal as a cover for aid to El Salvador, Liberal Congressional Democrats and moderate Republicans pressed the administration to varify that the government of El Salvador had fulfilled human rights conditions demanded by Congress before any aid can be received. Thus, both the authorization bill and the economic and military aid legislation the Reagan administration submitted in connection with the CBI provided opportunities for critics to attack his El Salvador policy (*Congressional Quarterly* 1982).

It should be noted also that the House Foreign Affairs Committee's version of the CBI bill stipulated that a minimum of $43.5 million of the authorized $350 be used for financing programs specifically aimed at development assistance in beneficiary countries. (At least $7.5 million and $2.0 million of this must be used, respectively, for scholarships in the U.S. and Inter-American Foundation programs in the Caribbean region).[19] Local currency should be generated from a minimum of 80% of the remaining $305.25 million which should be used to finance additional development programs. The bill further stipulated that the administration pursue a balance between assistance to the public and the private sectors, development aid, and balance of payments support in its use of funds authorized for CBI. And in what appears to be a prior agreement with the administration, the committee asked that particular emphasis be placed on those programs undertaken by private voluntary agencies, although it specified no dollar figure.

The Senate Foreign Relations Committee decided initially to transform the CBI bill into a multilateral assistance program. It adopted a motion by Senator Christopher Dodd (D-CN.) which would have changed the Administration's bilateral aid package into a multilateral program administered by the World Bank. The motion provided that the World Bank would put the CBI funds in a trust fund and use it to promote and finance development programs in the Caribbean under a management contract it would sign with the United States. The World Bank subsequently rejected this proposal. The Senate Foreign Relations vote to have CBI funds disbursed through the World Bank turned out to be an embarrassment not only to the Reagan administration but also to the committee's chairman Charles Percy (R-ILL.) Percy took the position that Dodd's World Bank amendment would diminish the impact of the aid. Percy also predicted correctly that the bank would not become involved (*Congressional Quarterly*, 1982). Sanford commented that the "enate panel's action suggested—that it had some serious reservations about the Administration's plans for emphasizing bilateral aid and diminishing the U.S. role in the Multilateral banks."[20] It became quite evident at a very early date that the U.S. Senate was in no particular hurry to deal with Reagan's Caribbean proposal. Hearings by the Foreign Relations Committee in April, 1982 drew very little attention to the aid request. Democrats on the panel showed by the questions they posed that they were at odds with the administration's sentiments in Latin America. Thus, the CBI proposal encountered delays both in the Senate's Finance and Foreign Relations Committees. The Finance Committee, which was responsible for the trade and tax provisions of the bill, had by the middle of May 1982 not yet conducted hearings. The Foreign Relations Committee had by the same time engaged in only one preliminary hearing, delaying any further debate on its portion of the bill until late May.

The Senate Foreign Relations panel, in a decision to change direction on its handling of the CBI legislation, sought on September 9 to expedite action on the program's 1982 fiscal year authorization by voting to report a new bill (S.2899). This bill was similar to the new House bill (H.R. 6755) which the House Foreign Affairs Committee had earlier reported and for which Congress had appropriated funds through the General Supplemental Appropriation Act. The essential difference in the Senate's bill involved language which reserved $10 million for programs managed by private voluntary organizations, while stipulating that the President exercise the necessary precaution to avoid any negative impact on U.S. agricultural producers from any production financed under the act. The Senate panel further added five new provisions to its version of the bill. The first, a "sense of the Congress" resolution proposed by Senator John Glenn (D-OH), sought a reconsideration by the Administration of its position regarding the pace of growth of the Inter-American Development Bank (IDB) lending with the possibility of some decrease. It also urged the administration to pursue a new IDB funding agreement whereby the Caribbean countries could secure a larger share, as much as 15 percent, of IDB loans in the future.[21]

The second provision requested that the Administration pay close attention to the possibility that the CBI plan would adversely affecting Puerto Rico and the Virgin Islands. A third provision noted that to the maximum extent possible Haiti's allocated portion of CBI funds should be administered through private voluntary organizations or the private sector. The fourth provision asked that more emphasis be placed on the tourism industry as a CBI component. Finally, the committee suggested that the President seek commitments from the Caribbean nations that they would help to protect the spawning grounds of the Western Atlantic bluefin tuna. In an effort to expedite matters due to the impending expiration of the fiscal year the Senate (in keeping with a similar action taken by the House) approved the $350 million in a supplemental appropriation bill, with the assurance that there would be ongoing consultation between the Administration and the Congress regarding the progress of the programs financed by the funds approved.

With regard to funding through the respective appropriations committees, the House subcommittee on Foreign Relations first decided to postpone action on the Administration's funding request for economic aid through the CBI program. A compromise was worked out, however, before the appropriations committee got ready to take the 1982 General Supplemental Appropriations bill (H.R. 6863) to the House floor. At this time the Congress, in addition to the CBI bill, was also considering a controversial administration proposal requesting $301 million in military assistance grants and loans. A compromise package was agreed on, containing $350 millon for the CBI (with a ceiling of $75 million in aid to El Salvador) and $52 million for military aid, all of which would be grants to the countries in the region except for El Salvador.[22]

In its version of the General Supplemental Appropriations Bill, the Senate Appropriations Committee voted full funding for the CBI, adding an additional $5 million for Honduras. This bill passed in the Senate without any significant controversy on August 11. Conferees from the House and Senate subsequently recommended that $350 million be appropriated for the CBI. Maximum as well as minimum amounts were set for country allocations such as a ceiling of $75 million for El Salvador and $10 million for Guatemala, a minimum of $20 million for the countries in the Eastern-Caribbean, and $41 million for the Dominican Republic. Also included were $10 million for Haiti, $50 million for Jamaica, $10 million for Belize, $70 million for Costa Rica, and $35 million for Honduras. Two million dollars was allocated for the American Institute for Free Labor, while another $2 million went to the Inter-American Foundation, leaving $25 million unallocated.[23]

Congress, on the urging of the Reagan administration approved the $350 million aid request in late 1982. The tax and trade components outlined in a separate package gained approval, with amendments by the House of Representatives, toward the end of 1982. In view of the fact that passage came late in the session, the bill was unable to reach the Senate floor prior to the expiration of the 97th Congress. Despite pressure from the Reagan administration, the Senate did not by the end of the session take any action on the trade portion of the CBI. On December 20, the Senate Finance Committee held an impromptu session to deal with the trade proposals (HR 7397). On December 21, the committee ordered H.R. 7397 favorably reported with amendments, (H.R. 7397 was passed by the House only three days earlier). An amendment by George Mitchell (D-ME), ensured protection to the U.S. textile industry by modifying a provision of the bill designed to help the Virgin Islands. Another amendment, by John Chafee (R-RI), altered a House provision that exempted a Virgin Island rum distillery from U.S. federal water polution controls. Finance Committee Chairman Robert Dole (R-KN), had earlier promised prompt action on the CBI. However, his panel did not begin to work on the bill until December 20. The trade plan for the CBI therefore effectively died in the Senate, at least for the 97th Congress (*Congressional Quarterly*, Dec. 1982).

President Reagan in his January 1983 State of the Union address before the 98th Congress stated that the "Final passage of the remaining portions" of the CBI was one of his administrations's "top legislative priorities for 1983."[24] The 98th Congress seemed somewhat more willing to respond to Reagan's urgings. The Senate Finance Committee granted approval on May 12, 1983 to the trade proposal of the CBI. The Senate had failed to act decisively on the proposal during the 97th Congress due largely to opposition from Sen. Russell B. Long, D-LA. Long, however, reversed his position and decided to support the bill. Thus, the Senate Finance Committee by a vote of 15-3 approved bill S 544. The full Senate added its version to HR 2973, a tax withholding bill, on June 16, after the House approved a separate version. The major difference between the Senate and House versions involved the question of rum imports and the need to protect the Virgin Islands rum trade. Finally on July 28 Congress passed the administration's special tax incentives (HR 2973). The Reagan administration had hoped for a broader program of trade and tax incentives. However, Congress concerned with the heavy burden of unemployment in the U.S. decreased the package. Though Reagan opposed the tax withholding legislation to which the Senate had attached the CBI, he nevertheless signed the bill on August 5 (*Congressional Quarterly Almanac*, 1983).

President Reagan had in a March 17, 1982 address to Congress noted that the political economic and security problems in the Caribbean Basin were formidable and that the countries in the region needed time to develop the necessary institutions conducive to a fee and democratic environment. Of significant importance, from the standpoint of understanding the early direction of Reagan's thoughts, is the fact that he stated that the countries in the Caribbean Basin region were in need of the means to defend themselves against what he considered "attempts by externally supported minorities to impose an alien, hostile and unworkable system upon them by force."[25]

The foregoing statement by Reagan is important as it demonstrates that, at least on the surface, the major elements of the CBI appear to support his administration's contention that its policies, with respect to the Third World in general and the Caribbean Basin region in particular, were sincere and benign. It makes the further claim that the administration was not, as charged, obsessed with the military and security dimensions of underdevelopment. However, as will be demonstrated later the CBI did not in scale, focus or intent merit as Payne has argued "comparison with the huge American effort to provide for the recovery of Europe after the Second World War." (Payne, 1988, p. 88).

Furthermore, it can be argued that the CBI's emphasis (although the State Department argued to the contrary) was not on, or aimed primarily at the dispensation of aid in the conventional sense, but rather on the elaboration of all available measures to stimulate the effective working of free enterprise in the region. Moreover, as events were later to confirm, the initiative was intended to discriminate politically between the countries in the region. As Payne put it, the CBI involved "rewarding friendly states like Jamaica under the JLP and punishing by exclusion states that were deemed to be too close to the Castro regime in Cuba" (Payne, 1988, p. 88). Indeed to many other analysts, (Pastor, 1982; Lowental, 1982; Gonzalez, 1982; Watson, 1985; Alexander, 1986), the CBI was specifically designed to foster and implement, in the strictest policy sense, the Reagan administration's strategy of ensuring "security through development" in a region it defines as one in which the U.S. has primary influence. Thus, the initiative became Washington's method of refocusing its attention on the Caribbean, a region previously neglected but having suddenly acquired a new sense of importance due primarily to the Marxist-Lennist threat perceived in the New Jewel Movement led by Maurice Bishop in Grenada and the Sandinista revolution led by Daniel Ortega in Nicaragua.

Notes

1. Mo Garica, "The Caribbean Aid Plan," United States International Communication Agency, July 14, 1981.

2. See Subcommittee on Oversight of the Committee on Ways and Means, U.S. House of Representative Report on CBI, May 6, 1987.

3. S1989 Guidebook: Caribbean BAsin Initiative U.S. Department of Commerce, International Trade Administration, U.S. and Foreign Commercial Service.

4. U.S. Department of Commerce, 1987 Guidebook: The Caribbean Basin Initiative (Washington D.C.: International Trade Administration, 1986)

5. *Congressional Digest*, 62: 69-96, March, 1983.

6. See, Congressional REsearch Service, Issue Brief #IB82074, CBI, Jonathan Sanford, 1983.

7. Ibid, p. 2

8. Ibid, p. 2

9. Lowenthal, Abraham F. 'Misplaced Emphasis' *Foreign Policy* No. 47, Summer 1982, p. 115.

10. Congressional Research Service, Issue Brief #1B82074, CBI, Jonathan Sanford, 1983.

11. Ibid, p. 5.

12. Ibid, p. 6.

13. Congressional Research Service (The Library of Congress) Caribbean Basin Initiative, IP0190C, April, 1982.

14. For a full account of the legislative process regarding the CBI see, The Caribbean Basin Initiative: Hearings and Markup before the Committee on Foreign Affairs and its Subcommittees on International Economic Policy and Trade and on Inter-American Affairs House of Representatives, 97th Congress, 2nd session on H.R. 5900. March 23, 25, 30; April 1, 27, 29; May 11; June 15, 1982. U.S. Government printing office, Washington: 1982.

15. Jonathan Sanford's Caribbean Basin Initiative: Issue Brief Number 1B82074, Library of Congress, 1982.

16. Ibid, p. 7.

17. Ibid, p. 7.

18. Ibid, p. 8.

19. Ibid, p. 8

20. Ibid, p. 9.

21. Ibid, p. 9.

22. Ibid, p. 10.

23. Ibid, p. 11.

24. Congressional Research Service, Issue Brief #1B82074, CBI, Jonathan Sanford 1983.

25. Ibid, p. 2

6
The Impact of the Caribbean Basin Initiative on the Jamaican Economy: Showpiece or Failure

The renewed interest in the Caribbean Basin and the heightened significance of this region within the context of United States global policy is seen by many analysts (Lowenthal, 1982; Gonzalez, 1982; Coleman and Herring, 1985; Deere, et al, 1990) as an awakening by the U.S. from what had previously been an approach bordering on benign neglect towards the countries in the region. This "awakening" subsequently led to the formulation and implementation of the CBI policy, encouraged by U.S. perceptions of a leftward political and ideological shift in the rhetoric and structure of a number of governments in the area. Specifically, the ideological and rhetorical orientation of the Michael Manley government in Jamaica and the growth and popularity of other "revolutionary" political movements in Nicaraqua, Guatemala, and El Salvador led the U.S. to begin a reappraisal of its policy. The expressed aim of the reappraisal was to "arrest" deteriorating economic and political conditions that were regarded as posing a threat to U.S. economic an security interests in the region.[1]

As noted earlier, the centerpiece of the CBI was one-way free trade. The U.S. would for the first time in the history of its policies in the region, offer a preferential trading arrangement. It would accord exports from the region duty-free treatment for a period of twelve years, the only exception being textiles and apparel—products that were manifestly crucial to the economies of the region. It justified the exception on the ground that these products were already affected by previous international agreements. CBI beneficiaries, however, would be accorded more liberal quotas. But, due to the exciegencies of U.S. politics, the Reagan administration had to ensure U.S. industry, agriculture, and labor that their interests would be protected against imports resulting from the CBI.

Indeed, almost immediately following the announcement of the initiative the Secretary of Agriculture John Block wasted no time in warning that agricultural commodities granted duty free entry to the U.S. from the Caribbean would be matched with an appropriate policy safeguard in the event such imports threaten to adversely affect the domestic economy.

An examination of the impact of the CBI on the economies of the Caribbean Basin states and Jamaica reveals that the primary objective was to continue existing U.S. policies and not to initiate a radical shift in policy. The CBI was, in the view of many analysts, a policy lacking in vision. For example, Abraham Lowenthal in an early analysis noted that "Despite all its positive features—the CBI leaves much to be desired." He found it particularly disturbing that "An East-West focus distorts every aspect of the CBI. The allocations for assistance suggest that obtaining aid from the United States will depend more on a country's attitude toward Cuba, U.S. foreign polices, and U.S. private investment than on the country's economic need or development prospects." Concluding on an even more somber note he pointed out that, "The CBI reflects the administration's interest in military security, political loyalty, and advantages for U.S. firms, rather than U.S. concern for the region's long-term development."[2]

Historically, the CBI is rooted in the U.S. desire to establish military hegemony in the region. Hegemony was the basic idea of the Monroe Doctrine of 1823, it dictated U.S. support (out of self-interest) for Cuba in the Spanish-American War of 1898, and it can be further seen in the Panama Canal Treaty of 1903, the Roosevelt-Corollary in 1904, and the Good Neighbor Policy of President Hoover in 1929. A similar U.S. initiative extending to all of Latin America resulted in the adoption and signing of the Inter-American Treaty of Reciprocal Assistance (The Rio Treaty) in 1947. The political-military aspect of hemispheric hegemony later acquired an economic dimension. U.S. security and economic interests were the basis of President Kennedy's Alliance for Progress initiated in 1961. The economic rationale for the Alliance for Progress should provide a better understanding of the CBI. President Kennedy persuaded Congress as well as the people of Latin America, the Caribbean and the United States that the Alliance would strengthen the economies of the countries in the hemisphere. He accomplished that task by invoking the memory of the success of the Marshall Plan. The Alliance did not meet its economic objectives, but U.S. security interests were maintained for the next two decades.

Twenty three years later President Ronald Reagan, ignoring the fact that the Alliance for Progress was an abject economic failure and that his Caribbean Basin Initiative was loaded with "hidden agendas", alluded to Kennedy's optimistic projections for the Alliance and asserted that the CBI would undoubtedly prove "that man's unsatisfied aspirations for economic progress and social justice can best be achieved by free men working within a framework of democratic institutions." Ironically, Reagan in utilizing excerpts from Kennedy's speech offered the Caribbean Basin Initiative as Gonzalez noted "as a successor to a failure—the Alliance for Progress."[3]

In order that one may gain a better understanding of the impact of the CBI on the economy of Jamaica and the Caribbean Basin countries, it is necessary to develop a more comprehensive analysis of the early indications regarding the direction CBI was designed to take. Tables 6.1 and 6.2 provide some basic economic information on the intended beneficiaries of the CBI while table 6.3 reveals the economic interest of the United States. It should be noted that the CBI is an integral part of U.S. foreign policy in the Latin American and Caribbean area. It was not designed nor was it implemented to aid primarily the economies of the targeted states as President Reagan and other supporters of the policy argued. The CBI was designed (as the mechanics of its implementation clearly indicate) to fulfill two primary purposes vital to the national interest of the United States. The first of these was to assist private enterprise, particularly U.S. businesses, by ensuring that the Caribbean region remain open to and safe for internal as well as external investments. Secondly, and of equal importance, to guarantee the economic and military security interests of the U.S. by ensuring its continued dominance of the western hemisphere.

With respect to the first of the two primary purposes of the CBI, it should be noted that Reagan administration spokesmen portrayed the initiative as geared toward support for private enterprise. Significantly, President Reagan in his message to Congress submitting the legislation authorizing the CBI. underlined the connection noting:

A key principle of the program is to encourage a more productive, competitive and dynamic private sector, and therefore provide the jobs, goods and services which the people of the Basin need for a better life for themselves and their children. All the elements of this program are designed to help establish the conditions under which a free competitive private sector can flourish.[4]

Supporters of the program for their part have consistently stressed the idea that the private sectors that will benefit from the initiative are those indigenous to the countries of the region:

The program—is integrated and designed to improve the lives of the

TABLE 6.1 U.S. Imports from CBERA-Designated Countries, 1983-1988 (in U.S.$ thousands)

	1983	1984	1985	1986	1987	1988
Antigua	8,809	7,898	24,695	11,849	8,621	6,893
Aruba[1]	—	—	—	1,797	2,452	647
Bahamas	1,676,394	1,154,282	626,084	440,985	377,881	268,328
Barbados	202,047	252,598	202,194	108,991	59,110	51,413
Belize	27,315	42,843	46,951	50,181	42,906	52,049
British Virgin Islands	880	1,335	11,902	5,904	11,162	684
Costa Rica	86,520	468,633	489,294	646,508	670,953	777,797
Dominica	242	86	14,161	15,185	10,307	8,530
Dominican Republic	806,520	994,427	965,847	1,058,927	1,144,211	1,425,371
El Salvador	58,898	381,391	395,658	371,761	272,881	282,584
Grenada	211	766	1,309	2,987	3,632	7,349
Guatemala	74,692	446,267	399,617	614,708	487,308	436,979
Guyana[2]	—	—	—	—	—	50,432
Haiti	337,483	377,413	386,697	368,369	393,660	382,466
Honduras	364,742	393,769	370,219	430,906	483,096	439,504
Jamaica	262,360	396,949	267,016	297,891	393,912	440,934
Montserrat	924	989	3,620	3,472	2,413	2,393
Netherlands Antilles[1]	2,274,510	2,024,367	793,162	453,330	478,836	408,100
Panama[3]	336,086	311,627	393,605	352,206	342,700	256,046
St. Kitts-Nevis[4]	18,758	23,135	16,258	22,278	23,793	20,822
St. Lucia	4,700	7,397	13,796	12,269	17,866	26,044
St. Vincent-Grenadines	4,276	2,958	9,643	7,836	8,493	13,950
Trinidad-Tobago	1,317,534	1,360,106	1,255,498	786,405	802,838	701,738
Total	8,763,900	8,649,235	6,687,226	6,064,745	6,039,030	6,061,054

Source: U.S. International Trade Commission, *Annual Report on the Impact of the Caribbean Basin Economic Recovery Act on U.S. Industries and Consumers*, Fourth Report, 1988 (Washington, D.C.: USTIC, 1989), table 1.3.

1) Aruba's designation as a CBERA beneficiary became effective on January 1, 1986. For statistical purposes, Aruba had been treated as part of the Netherlands Antilles until separate data became available.
2) Guyana was not designated a beneficiary until November 24, 1988.
3) Panama lost its designation as a beneficiary on April 19, 1988, but then regained it in December 1989.
4) Anguilla, which has not been designated as a beneficiary country, had been included with the data for St. Kitts-Nevis through 1985.

TABLE 6.2 U.S. Economic Assistance to the Caribbean Basin, 1980-1989[1]
(U.S. $ thousands)

	1980	1981	1982	1983	1984	1985	1986	1987	1988	1989
Belize	0	0	0	17	4	22	9	13	7	8
Dominican Republic	35	7	60	35	64	125	66	20	32	20
Haiti	11	9	12	27	26	31	46	74	31	28
Jamaica	3	54	119	82	88	115	83	42	19	77
Regional	45	27	50	58	105	58	49	51	33	29
Subtotal—Caribbean	94	107	241	219	287	350	253	200	122	162
Costa Rica	14	11	32	184	145	181	131	160	102	100
El Salvador	52	78	155	199	161	373	261	364	266	253
Guatemala	8	9	8	22	5	71	85	150	110	114
Honduras	46	26	68	87	71	199	105	173	130	53
Nicaragua	19	58	6	0	0	0	0	0	0	5
Panama	1	9	12	6	11	69	24	8	1	0
Regional Programs[2]	4	11	13	19	15	160	72	20	54	61
Subtotal—Central America	144	202	294	517	408	1057	678	875	663	586
Total Caribbean Basin	238	309	535	736	695	1402	931	1075	785	748

Source: Agency for International Development, *Congressional Presentation Fiscal Year 1985*, Annex III, pp. 2–3; *Congressional Presentation Fiscal Year 1987*, Main Volume, pp. 438–40, 479–81; *Congressional Presentation Fiscal Year 1988*, Main Volume, pp. 509, 512, 517; *Congressional Presentation Fiscal Year 1989* and *1990*, Summary Tables.

1) Development Assistance and Economic Support Funds only
2) Includes ROCAP

TABLE 6.3 Investment Incentives in the Caribbean, 1986

	Free Trade Zones	Tax Holiday	Import Duty Exemption	Profit Repatriation	Double Tax Relief
Antigua-Barbuda	—	10-15 yrs.	on raw materials & machines	no restrictions	—
Aruba	1	10-11 yrs.	granted	—	granted
Belize	1 Industrial park, another under construction	10-15 yrs.	on raw materials & machines for export production	no restrictions	granted
British Virgin Islands	—	10 yrs.	granted	no restrictions	granted
Dominica	planning export processing zone	10-15 yrs.	on raw materials & machines for export production	almost no restrictions	granted
Dominican Republic	4 export processing zones; 2 Industrial parks under construction	8-20 yrs.	granted	no restrictions	granted
Grenada	Industrial park under construction	10-15 yrs.	no restrictions if from CARICOM sources	no restrictions	granted
Haiti	yes[1]	5-20 yrs.	some restrictions	no restrictions	granted
Jamaica	2 export processing zones; 1 to begin operations	5-10 yrs.	granted	no restrictions	granted
Montserrat	—	10-15 yrs.	—	no restrictions	granted
St. Lucia	yes[1]	10-15 yrs.	—	some restrictions on non-residents	granted
St Vincent-Grenadines	1 industrial park, another planned	10-15 yrs.	granted	no restrictions	granted
Trinidad-Tobago	—	—	granted	no restrictions	granted

Source: Caribbean/Central American Action, *Country Profiles* (Washington D.C.:C/CAA, 1986).
[1] Number of free trade zones or export processing zones not reported
— Information not reported.

TABLE 6.3A Share of Exports to and Imports from Selected Caribbean Countries, 1961-63 and 1983-85

	% of Exports to the U.S.		% of Imports from the U.S.	
	Average 1961-63	Average 1983-85	Average 1961-63	Average 1983-85
Bahamas	91.7	84.0	56.4	52.7
Barbados	6.7	52.7	14.7	45.8
Dominican Republic	74.1	73.3	47.4	34.5
Guyana	18.7	25.0	21.2	21.7
Haiti	54.4	79.9	57.9	69.4
Jamaica	36.0	39.1	27.7	42.8
Suriname	n.a.	24.1	n.a.	32.6
Trinidad-Tobago	25.7	60.5	13.3	40.9

Source: Inter-American Development Bank, *Economic and Social Progress in Latin America*, Annual Report 1987 (Washington D.C.: IDB, 1987), p. 126.

peoples of the Caribbean Basin by enabling them to earn their own way to a better future. It builds on the principles of integrating aid, self-help and participation in trade and investments.[5]

From a practical standpoint, however, the implementation of the CBI raises questions about the proponents assumptions with respect to the private sectors which stand to benefit. Indeed, Zorn and Mayerson noted in one of the earliest analyses of the CBI that "The private sector which it will support is that based in the United States."[6] Other analysts have argued that the CBI is much more than a single piece of financial legislation. Rather it is a very broad policy directive which has brought to bear the full weight and influence of the U.S. government on the economies of the countries in the Caribbean Basin (Deere, et al, 1990, p. 154). In fact there is to date a strong consensus within the Caribbean community that the CBI is a policy designed specifically to implement the Reagan administration's concept of a new political and economic order in the Caribbean. Such a new order would ensure "security through development" in an area long considered "America's backyard", created and sustained by the Monroe Doctrine (Deere et al, 1990, p. 154).

While many critics viewed the CBI as a cover to mask U.S. military escalation in the area,[7] Jamaica's Prime Minister Edward Seaga, the original architect of the idea (though in entirely different terms), embraced the initiative as the vehicle that would propel Jamaica's and the region's economy toward a much brighter future. Jamaica became in the eyes of the Reagan administration the "Showcase" through which the "magic" of the policy's objectives would be demonstrated. The government of Jamaica saw in the program an opportunity to influence the trade and aid patterns in the area; moving from dependence on foreign aid in the form of grants and loans to a position of self-reliance based on joint development projects. In the almost mad rush to embrace the glowing promises of the CBI, Jamaican and other Caribbean leaders failed to see that the fundamental premise evident in the economic offerings of the policy was hidden in what Deere et al, described as "the alleged promise of laissez faire", (Deere, et al, 1990, p. 155).

Seaga and the JLP government accepted the Reagan administration's contention that the opening up of markets in the United States that were traditionally closed or restricted to the region's products would contribute to a dramatic increase in investments leading to increased employment opportunities, higher income earnings, and expanding trade. An increased capacity to generate foreign exchange, it was argued, would result from the increase in trade allowing the countries in the region confronted with severe external debt problems to adequately meet their debt-service commitments. Further analysis shows, however, that the emphasis placed on the laissez-faire model as an avenue for economic development has proven to be anything other than the panacea Seaga expected it to be. Indeed, the evidence reveals that rather than opening up vast markets for Caribbean products the CBI, as was intended, initiated the effective restructuring of U.S.-Caribbean economic relations. It has significantly tied the region more closely to United States corporate interests and as such has improved the international competitive position of U.S. industries.

Although the CBI attempted to stimulate exports from the Caribbean Basin countries, it also encouraged greater imports to them from the U.S., thereby ensuring an increase in sales at a time when U.S. products no longer enjoy a position of dominance in world markets. Analysts have argued that the Reagan administration's decision to engage the debt crisis problem with a strategy linked to a new system of trade agreements evolved as a result of an understanding that both borrowers and creditors were caught in the debt trap (Deere, 1990, et al, p. 155). Bearing in mind the foregoing, it becomes evident that the CBI provided U.S. multinational corporations many advantages that were not available in the special tariff programs already in existence such as the General System of Preferences (GSP), which gives the president the authority to grant duty free treatment to eligible products from Third World countries for a period of ten years. Of particular importance were sections 806.3 and 807 of the Special Tariff Provisions of the CBI which provide special duty treatment for imports containing U.S. components.

In addition, the eligibility criteria stipulated for CBI beneficiary status were specifically designed to ensure privileged access for U.S. capital to Caribbean markets. Countries designated as beneficiaries can jeopardize that status by simply allowing for the preferential entry of products from other countries classified as developed, if such products adversely affect U.S. trade with the beneficiary country. Eligibility status can also be affected if the country nationalized, expropriated or assumed control of U.S. owned property. This provision was included in the CBI despite an ongoing difference in the interpretation of International Law between the U.S. and Third World countries regarding the right of a country to control economic or other foreign owned entities within its sovereign territory. Finally, eligibility status is threatened if the designated country decides not to cooperate with the U.S. in the control of narcotics.[8] Thus, it is evident that the CBI was designed, at least in part, as a vehicle to ensure U.S. political and economic dominance in the region.

Deere et al, further note that other forms of beneficiary designation left to presidential discretion such determinations as whether a designated country agrees to "provide equitable and reasonable access to its markets and basic resources to the United States; the degree to which a beneficiary country uses export subsidies or imposes export performance requirements or local content requirements that could distort international trade; and the degree to which workers' rights are protected" (Deere et al, 1990, p. 156).

The fundamental objectives of the CBI were manifest early in the development of the policy. However, Prime Minister Seaga, because of Jamaica's precarious economic position resulting in large measure from adverse

U.S. reaction to the militancy of the Manley era, embraced fully the CBI and led the country into the "protective arms of the U.S." As Payne observed, Seaga exerted a considerable amount of effort to please the U.S. and was accordingly "rewarded with increased aid, an easing of trade barriers, and political support in dealing with the International Monetary Fund."[9]

Seaga worked hard to convince other countries in the region to reject the "Pro-Cuban" model of socialist development, condemned the revolutionary governments of Grenada and Nicaragua, and strongly encouraged a stronger U.S. role in the Caribbean Basin region. In short he came to be known as "America's man in the Caribbean".[10] However, the realities of the CBI policy in terms of its impact on the economy of Jamaica were soon felt. It began with the reduction of the Island's sugar quota by almost 46 percent. Between 1983 and 1986 sugar imports from Jamaica to the United States decreased from U.S. $14.92 million to U.S. $2.35 million.[11] In a speech to the Jamaican business community (with a visiting U.S. Congressional delegation in attendance), Deputy Prime Minister and Minister of Foreign Affairs Hugh Shearer emphasized the extent of the impact of the CBI on the Jamaican economy by noting that the quota even restricted the "imports of Milo, a chocolate-based beverage exported to the West Indian ethnic market in the United States." The minister further noted that products that include sugar even with a low sugar content, were often subject to the sugar quota for Jamaica.[12]

The U.S. Agriculture and Food Act of 1981 called for the support of sugar prices each year at minimum specified levels. When sugar prices fell, President Reagan reintroduced an import quota system in 1982 aimed at maintaining high domestic prices. As a result the 1985 Food Security Act required that the sugar program be administered at no cost to the U.S. Treasury. What followed was a drastic reduction in the U.S. imports of sugar from 5 million short tons in 1980-81 to about 1 million tons in 1987 (Deere, et al, 1990). Overall the sugar import quota for the Caribbean Basin countries declined from an average annual 1.6 million tons in 1979-81 to 268,000 tons in 1987. Since the Caribbean Basin Economic Recovery Act (CBERA) came into force a 78 percent quota reduction has reduced potential sugar export earnings of the Caribbean Basin in the 1984-88 period by as much as $500 million. At the end of 1990, it was estimated that some 120,000 jobs were lost in the Caribbean as a result of a diminishing U.S. sugar import quota. Jamaica's experience resulting from these reductions has been devastating (Deere, et al, 1990, p. 161).

Other forms of agricultural exports to the U.S. from Jamaica also experienced significant reductions. Many of these resulted from the barriers erected by the U.S. Department of Agriculture. For example, "Ackee", a vegetable locally grown in Jamaica, although exported without difficulty to the EEC countries, was refused entry to U.S. markets. Citrus products, a traditional export to the U.S. were suddenly barred by the USDA on the assumption that Jamaican citrus carried a fruit disease. By the time it was determined that citrus products from Jamaica did not carry any "fruit disease", the massive losses incurred by the industry proved to be too severe for an attempt to be made to revitalize the industry. Anticipating an increase in non-traditional agricultural exports to the U.S. as a result of the CBI, the Seaga government implemented in early 1984 a structural adjustment program designed to broaden the base of sectoral earnings of foreign exchange and specifically to reduce reliance on the earnings of the mining sector. The basic plan implemented with special regard to agriculture is called the National Plan of Agricultural Development or Agro-21. This program is targeted at the rehabilitation and expansion of traditional export crops and the development of non-traditional crops and agribusiness opportunities to further increase export potentials.

Although created by the public sector the agricultural development plan is designed to be implemented by the private sector. A number of projects geared to exploit the export potential of the CBI were started under the 'Agro-21' plan including major developments in the cultivation of fresh fruits, vegetables and flowers among others. It was optimistically estimated that these non-traditional export crops would realize a 7.5 percent increase in exports per year in real terms. The benefits expected from the agricultural development venture have not materialized. Indeed while nearly 200,000 acres were earmarked for this project less than 100,000 acres were committed as it became evident at an early date that agricultural products-especially non-traditional crops-would suffer the same fate as sugar and citrus in attempts to enter the U.S. market. The adverse impact and loss in potential earnings in the agricultural sector led the former Deputy Prime Minister, Hugh Shearer, to complain that the arbitrary and inconsistent policy rulings by the U.S. Customs Service adversely affected exports from Jamaica and other CBI beneficiary countries resulting in the loss of millions of dollars in orders (*Jamaica Weekly Gleaner*, December 14, 1987). Indeed the crippling restrictions imposed on the principal exports from the Island is often referred to as the reason for the disappointing performance of the CBI.

Jamaican exporters have had to deal with unanticipated problems that their products have faced at U.S. ports of entry. Attention has primarily focused on the U.S. Customs Service and USDA. On a continuing basis exporters have detailed "horror stories" about the trouble they encounter in satisfying USDA standards and regulations in their efforts to gain entry for their products. Correspondingly they point to the role of the Customs Service in response to U.S. lobbyists, introducing quarantine requirements, reclassifying certain products and in other ways effectively banning goods that the U.S. Congress had not specifically sought to exclude from the U.S. market. They also note that the ambiguities and confusion that result from the scarcity of information available in Jamaica on these policies are as troubling as the exclusions themselves. A major cause of uncertainty is the power of the U.S. President under the CBI to terminate, upon the recommendation of the Secretary of Commerce, trade preferences for designated products. Jamaican producers argue that such a stipulation can and has caused considerable dislocations.[13]

The manufacturing sector in Jamaica has not in itself benefited much from the CBI except, as will be noted, the case of textiles in recent times. The growth of manufacturing based on external investments and the subsequent increase in trade held much promise in its potential scope and benefit to Jamaica and the Caribbean Basin region. Both have proven to be quite limited due in part to the dilution of the CBERA legislation by Congress. Moreover, the investment tax incentive which was eliminated left no direct workable mechanism capable of stimulating investment in the region. Compounding the situation is the fact that a number of trade exclusions were included in or added to the legislation resulting in the exclusion of some of the more vitally important export products from the potential benefits of free trade (Deere, et al, 1990, p. 158). The products excluded were textiles and apparel, selected leather products and footwear, canned tuna, petroleum, and petroleum derivatives. It should be noted that in 1983 crude petroleum and petroleum products were the leading exports from the Caribbean, with textiles and apparel the second leading manufactured item.

The significant loss to Jamaica and the Caribbean region can be seen in the fact that had textiles and apparel been included in the CBERA legislation from the initiation of the policy an estimated increase of about 285% in related trade benefits could have been realized. Deere, et al, noted that the foregone benefits were of that magnitude because the industries involved "are subject to relatively high tariffs (around 25 percent) as well as quotas." They estimate the value of the exclusions to be comparable to the total non sugar trade assigned free-trade privileges under the CBI (approximately U.S. $400 million) (Deere et al, 1990, p. 160). President Reagan announced in 1986 a "special access program" aimed at increasing quotas for specific apparel imported from CBI designated countries (See Table 6.1).

President Reagan's special access program, called the 807-A facility, applies only to garment items assembled in the region after being cut in the United States from U.S. manufactured fabric. An interesting aspect of this facility is that bilateral agreements would have to be negotiated by the CBI beneficiaries, which in turn would determine the guaranteed access levels (GALS) to which the respective countries can aspire. This is independent of normal quotas applied to other textiles and garments covered under section 807 of the Special Tariff Provisions.[14] Exports to the U.S. under 807-A, as under 807, continue to pay duty on the Caribbean value-added component. By 1989 only a total of five Caribbean nations had signed bilateral agreements with the U.S. with the intention of taking advantage of that benefit, these are Jamaica, Trinidad and Tobago, Haiti, Costa Rico and the Dominican Republic.[15]

CBI results have to date shown that the most noticeable growth, "128 percent between 1983 and 1988" has been primarily in manufacturing exports, led in part by two product categories that are excluded from CBERA provisions, garments and leather products. Correspondingly, the export performance of chemicals and pharmaceutical, electronics, sporting goods, and methyl and ethyl alcohol has been very unstable (Deere, et al, 1990, p. 167). Consequently it can be argued that the most visible gain as far as Jamaica and some other Caribbean beneficiaries are concerned with regard to the CBERA provisions has been in textiles and apparel, a sector that is excluded from CBERA benefits, but benefits from section 807 of the tariff code. Textile and apparel have registered the most gain of all other manufacturing exports. Although excluded from CBERA benefits these two imports into the United States from the region registered an annual growth of 28 % between 1983 and 1986, actually increasing to 39% in 1987. Deere, et al, noted that this impressive growth is partially due to the GALS program. Under 807-A special access apparel imports totalled U.S. $162 million in 1988, a little less than 11 percent of total imports of textiles and apparels (Deere et al, 1990).[16]

In the area of investment promotion with regard to access to the U.S. markets the Jamaican business interests have not fared well in spite of the CBI. At the very top of the list of complaints from the business community is the problem of investment promotion and the inability to penetrate U.S. markets. Indeed these two areas have been prominently identified as the primary impediments to taking advantage of the limited opportunities offered by the CBI. To be sure the question has been raised as to whether the Jamaican industrial entity can provide adequate quantities and assure deliveries on a timely basis. The Jamaican business community in answer to that question points to the inadequacy of U.S. AID funding for investment promotion activities. They also complain that the eligibility criteria to qualify as a CBI beneficiary are specifically designed to create privileged access for U.S. capital to the Jamaican as well as the Caribbean market. It points to the fact that Congress diluted considerably the CBERA legislation, effectively eliminating the investment tax incentive, thus leaving no direct mechanism to stimulate investment.

As in the case of textiles and apparel the Jamaican tourism industry showed some improvement, although the contribution of the CBI to that increase is minimal. In 1985 World Bank estimates were that Jamaica's gross national product (GNP) per head, measured at average 1983-85 prices, was U.S. $940. According to these estimates, in the period 1965-85, GNP per head declined in real terms by an average of 0.7% per year. Understandably tourism has become the major source of Jamaica's foreign exchange. While the years 1978 and 1979 were extremely profitable for tourism, the industry began a steady decline in 1980, stemming from political unrest in Kingston, Jamaica's capital city. By 1981, the industry began to show some recovery. This continued in 1982, partly due to a U.S. $12 million foreign advertising campaign undertaken by the government of Jamaica. In the winter season of 1982, tourist arrivals increased by approximately 60 percent to 650,000. A further 21 percent increase was recorded in 1983. This continued into 1984 with arrivals reaching a total of 843,775.[17]

Gross earnings from tourism rose to U.S. $435 million in 1984 from $399 million in 1983, but fell to $406.8 million in 1985. In 1986, however, earnings totaled approximately U.S. $500 millon. Between January and June 1987, these earnings showed a 17% increase over the total for the first six months of 1986.[18] However, despite an early optimism regarding the impact of CBI on the tourism industry it soon became apparent that the industry stood to benefit very little if at all from the initiative. Early optimism turned to pessimism when it was discovered that CBI beneficiaries had to sign a Tax Information Exchange Agreement (TIEA) with the U.S. before the convention tax benefit provision of the agreement could apply. The convention tax benefit would allow U.S. taxpayers to legitimately deduct business expenses incurred in attending a business meeting or convention in Jamaica or any other qualifying CBI country without regard to the more stringent requirements usually applied to foreign convention expenses.

As a standard practice even before the inception of the CBI, expenses incurred at conventions held in the "North American area" are generally deductible by U.S. taxpayers while those incurred at conventions outside the area generally are not. The Caribbean Basin Economic Recovery Act included CBI beneficiary countries in the "North American area" definition, for those who sign the TIEA with the U.S. Treasury. To date, only Jamaica, Barbadoes, St. Lucia and Dominica have signed TIEAs and the prospect that many more CBI designated countries will sign are not good. The principal objections to such agreements are that they allow too much foreign intrusion into the private affairs of domestic residents and that the reciprocal nature of the agreements give Caribbean governments too much power to look into the U.S. business affairs of Caribbean residents. Furthermore, the economic losses from giving up financial privacy would be greater than any potential gain from the convention business (and since the Tax Reform Act of 1986, from any borrowing from 936 funds).[19]

When the Tax Information Exchange Agreement was first announced, senior members of the tourism business community, cognizant of the heavy losses incurred by the industry during the Michael Manley administration, and now apparently willing to "grab at straws," argued that this benefit would help CBI countries attract U.S. business meetings and conventions which would in turn boost tourism earnings. Jamaica's experience to date, however, with the convention tax benefit is that the gains have been negligible. Confidential interviews conducted by the author with senior government officials in the Ministry of Tourism as well as the Jamaican Tourist Board has confirmed these findings. The increases shown in the tourism industry since the inception of the CBI are attributed exclusively to the efforts of the government through its aggressive "make it Jamaica Again" advertising campaign.[20] The primary argument against repeal of the TIEA requirement, apart from the embarrassment of admitting failure, is that it would undermine those countries which have cooperated with the U.S. and have signed the TIEAs while giving the appearance of rewarding those countries with competing convention destinations which have not cooperated.

In the area of trade performance, a closer examination of Jamaica's experience reveals that its overall experience up to the present has not been overly satisfactory. In the first two years of the initiative Jamaica's trade figures indicated a 3.5 percent decline in exports to the United States (due in part to bauxite and alumina). For CBI beneficiary countries the decline was a disappointing 23.1% (see Table 6.2). Marginal supporters of the initiative argue that while it would be easy to conclude from the "evidence" that the CBI is a failure, a closer focus on disaggrated statistics offers a more "encouraging picture." Jerry Haar points to trade analyst Craig Van Grasstek's findings, which he believes offers a more accurate picture of the trade performance of the Caribbean Basin countries. This he accomplishes by separating the designated countries of the region into subregions for trade performance analysis.[21] It is argued that the 23.1% decline in imports between 1983 and 1985 was attributable primarily to the steep declines in U.S. imports from two of the three oil refining countries.

Despite the optimism displayed by Haar and Van Grasstek in their analyses, the evidence shows that whatever gains may have occurred from the CBI were offset by the sharp drop in prices of traditional exports, Jamaica being no exception. It suffered severe economic dislocation with bauxite and alumina exports dropping even further in 1986 (see Table 6.4). The negative effects of the decline in traditional exports were not balanced by the CBI because the tax incentives designated to make private investment in Jamaica attractive were cut by Congress. Many development experts argue that the fundamental problem with the CBI is that the program was conceived and formulated more to satisfy United States needs and interests than the needs and interests of Jamaica in particular or the Caribbean region in general. Many senior government and bureaucracy officials in Jamaica have privately expressed to the author the opinion that the emphasis on making the region attractive to United States business and security interests has come at the expense of efforts to develop local skills and industries.

Development analyst Stephen Hellinger argues that the CBI "has not built on the productive strength of the region" pointedly adding that instead the program encourages offshore production, such as the assembling of electronic components, that creates little stable employment and has few backward linkages into the local economies.[22] Stewart Tucker of the Overseas Development Council echoes the views of many in the region by noting that "the only way you're going to radically change the economies in the region is with major new

TABLE 6.4 Gross Domestic Product (Constant Prices) ($'000)

	1982	1983	1984	1985r	1986p
I. Goods	679.17	703.79	694.69	652.29	667.70
Agriculture, Forestry and Fishing	143.77	154.25	168.56	162.78	159.58
Export Agriculture	24.42	23.65	24.48	23.74	23.06
Domestic Agriculture	69.22	75.19	87.05	85.66	82.21
Livestock Hunting & Fishing	41.28	46.13	47.50	43.28	43.06
Forestry and Logging	8.86	9.27	9.53	10.10	11.24
Mining and Quarrying	116.99	117.67	118.52	95.35	101.65
Bauxite and Alumina	112.36	112.77	113.80	91.79	97.93
Other Mining	4.63	4.90	4.72	3.56	3.71
Manufacturing	303.70	309.45	293.92	296.69	305.77
Construction and Installation	114.71	122.42	113.70	97.47	100.71
II. Services	1,295.46	1,325.59	1,300.39	1,249.64	1,313.28
Basic Services	151.40	160.53	164.63	167.92	183.56
Electricity and Water	24.63	26.81	26.84	27.50	31.32
Transport, Storage and Communication	126.77	133.72	137.79	140.42	152.24
Other Services	1,144.06	1,165.06	1,135.76	1,081.72	1,129.72
Distributive Trades	311.19	295.63	292.86	273.18	288.77
Financial Institutions	115.45	140.16	128.82	115.84	141.30
Real Estate Services	229.49	236.18	232.05	227.54	233.16
Producers of Government Services	368.64	370.35	357.91	338.06	332.10
Miscellaneous Services	99.46	102.86	103.68	106.20	112.00
Households and Private Non-Profit	19.84	19.88	20.44	20.91	22.59
III. Less: Imputed Service Charges	76.87	88.17	70.91	64.96	104.50
TOTAL GROSS DOMESTIC PRODUCT	1,897.76	1,941.21	1,924.16	1,836.97	1,876.48

rRevised
pPrimary
Source: Statistical Institute of Jamaica.

amounts of U.S. aid for economic development." The prospect of more economic aid flowing into the area has been dealt a blow by the severe cuts imposed by Congress for budgetary reasons.[23] Despite these cuts, however, Jamaica by aligning is policies with the United States was able to attract large-scale U.S. economic assistance along with support for loans and grants from international agencies. This support came as a result of the strong ideological alliance between Jamaican Prime Minister Edward Seaga and President Ronald Reagan. The bulk of assistance to Jamaica consisted of balance of payments support (Economic Support Funds) instead of project oriented developmental assistance. This assistance was conditioned on the Seaga government instituting changes in Jamaica's economic policy as prescribed by the IMF.

As indicated in table 6.5 Jamaica received extensive U.S. foreign assistance during the Seaga administration. This assistance differed from the proposed benefits that were to be derived from the CBI. Between 1980 when the Seaga government came to power, and 1982, U.S. aid to Jamaica increased from U.S. $14.6 million to U.S. $140.7 million. It is estimated that during the seven years of the Seaga administration, Jamaica averaged among the top 20 recipients of U.S. aid. Libby noted that Jamaica's top 20 rating is figured "out of roughly 115 recipient countries." He also noted that:

> Jamaica ranked within the top 10 U.S. aid recipients if the figures are calculated on a per capita basis. For example, in 1985 Jamaica ranked number 15 out of 116 recipients or number 5 on a per capita basis. This high level of U.S. economic assistance continued. For example, during fiscal year 1987, estimated U.S. assistance to Jamaica of U.S. $86.5 million placed it number 17 out of 115 aid recipients and the congressionally requested figure for 1988 of U.S. $107.8 would place Jamaica 16 out of 116 recipients (Libby, 1990, p. 103).

However, the massive U.S. assistance referred to had very little positive impact on the economic problems of the Island.

In addition, it is argued that the involvement of the IMF affected adversely the overall economic picture. This can be understood in view of the fact that the aim of the IMF assistance, which is accompanied by conditions pertaining to fiscal policies, is structural adjustment or economic stabilization that enables Jamaica to better service its external debt. IMF aid is not designed primarily to build up foreign currency reserves or enhance internal economic development.

Proponents of the CBI aid package argue that it was tied to IMF prescriptions because the basic strategic aim is the improvement of the Island's export performance, with an emphasis on encouraging the development of non-traditional exports eligible for duty free treatment under the CBERA. Moreover, U.S. aid strategy regards economic policy reform as the key to effective use of external resources. U.S. assistance would be designed to

TABLE 6.5 Refinancing Jamaica's External Debt (U.S. $ millions)

Source of Loans	December 1980 Loan	%	July 1984 Loan	%	Percent Change
World Bank	97.8	11.3	325.8	19.2	+232.1
Inter-American Development Bank	48.2	5.6	105.0	6.2	+117.8
USAID	46.1	5.3	387.1	22.8	+739.7
Commercial Banks	351.1	40.6	512.3	30.2	+45.9
Other	321.9	37.2	365.6	21.6	+13.5
Total	$865.1	100.0	$1,695.8	100.0	

SOURCE: *Daily Gleaner* (November 30, 1984).

promote structural reform and long-run development. However, the massive inflow of U.S. aid funds to Jamaica ended up having a minimal effect on the economic problems faced by the Seaga government.

Public officials and private sector business leaders in Jamaica have expressed concern and disappointment over the performance of the CBI since its inception. They point to such examples as section 423 of the Tax Reform Act of 1986 which amended the 1983 CBI legislation by imposing restrictions on the duty-free treatment of ethanol imports from CBI countries, as an indication of U.S. policy to protect domestic industris from Caribbean competition. In addition to the restriction on ethanol imports Jamaican government officials cite provisions in continuing budget resolutions. For example, in 1987 H.J. Resolution 738, barred the U.S. Travel and Tourism Administration of the Department of Commerce from funding activities, such as policy studies or technical assistance, that could benefit the tourism industry in Jamaica. The same resolution restricted the International Trade Administration of the Department of Commerce and the U.S. Agency for International Development from engaging in or funding programs that publicize the advantages of relocating U.S. business overseas. In addition, 1987 continuing resolution specifically disallowed any funding that would finance the development of foreign agricultural exports which could compete with U.S. production.[24]

This analysis of the impact of the trade, investment, and aid components of the CBI on the economy of Jamaica leads to the conclusion that their overall effects, while positive, have been extremely limited. These limitations are characteristic of the overall performance of the CBI. A similar conclusion, of negligible impact, must be drawn for the Caribbean Basin region in general.

The social consequences of the CBI are also important. Deere, et al, in their analysis of the CBI point to the emphasis placed on the private sector and they noted that U.S. private business interests are the largest beneficiaries of the CBI. They also observed that development assistance is almost exclusively focused on the private sector "allegedly to ameliorate constraints to trade and investment expansion in the region" (Deere, et al, 1990, p. 176) They further note that this focus came at the direct expense of government programs vitally needed to help improve the living standards of the poor. Social development in all its ramifications was overlooked by the CBI in order to shower incentives on the private sector with the expressed aim of increased export, thus allowing governments to repay their external debts. There is, however, a larger picture with regard to the underlying concept of the CBI that must be scrutinized which is the political and security aspects of United States policy in the Caribbean Basin region. As soon as the CBI program was announced by President Reagan, critics argued that the initiative was a "mask" behind which the government of the United States intended to significantly increase its military involvement in the Caribbean Basin (Zorn and Mayerson, 1983; Lowenthal, 1982; Weintraub, 1982; Fienberg and Newfarmer, 1982; Watson, 1982, 1985).

Of vital importance is the fact that Deere, et al, in 1990, eight years after the implementation of the CBI, echoed and confirmed the fears of the early critics with regard to the military intentions of the U.S. government in the Caribbean Basin region. They found that U.S. military assistance has sharply increased in the region in concert with the CBERA. Military assistance to the Caribbean area took a significant leap between 1982 and 1984, and as Deere et al note it "almost doubled again the next year, peaking in 1985 at $46.5 million" (Deere, et al, 1990, p. 176) (See Table 6.6).

Of course, a strong U.S. military presence in the Caribbean is not a new phenomon. The Cuban revolution of 1959 coupled with what the U.S. regards as a state of "political and social instability" in the region have in the view of the U.S. State and Defense Departments troubling consequences and as such are cause for alarm. Since the 1962 Cuban Missile crisis the U.S. military presence, had assumed a much lower profile. President Carter, in response to the revolutions in Nicaragua and Grenada and to a decrease in emphasis on isolating Cuba by many Latin American and Caribbean countries sought to reassert U.S. military power in the Caribbean. Carter's attempt to redefine U.S. military policy in the Caribbean was, however, mild in comparison with the position taken by President Reagan. The Reagan administration perused a vigorous policy of arms and aid with the lines between the two at times extremely blurred. Some analysts (Watson, 1985) argue that revolutionary movements and the regimes they create, as well as the "entire phenomenon of the national liberation revolution" are by definition a serious challenge to U.S. power. The Caribbean Basin Initiative is therefore seen by Watson as "a classic and concrete assertion of the purpose of American power in the Western Hemisphere." Watson further remarks that what America is seeking to accomplish at this time has to do with reasserting a weakened hegemony." (Watson, 1985, p. 13)

In concert with CBERA policy, President Reagan vigorously pursued a parallel policy aimed at increasing U.S. military power in the region along with the promotion and coordination of indigenous security forces. The large scale military maneuvers or "war games" conducted in the Caribbean between 1981 and 1984 followed close on the inauguration of Reagan. In his campaign speeches Reagan left no doubt as to the direction his military policy in the Caribbean would take. Thus, it can be argued the objective of these military manuevers among other things, was to pressure Cuba. "By 1984", Deere et al observe, "there were twenty-one U.S. military installations in the Caribbean Basin, 30,000 U.S. troops, plus another 10,000 shipborne troops" (Deere, et al, 1990, p. 178). The stated objective of the manuevers and increased U.S. military assistance, according to the Reagan administration, was to construct a security system based on U.S. military equipment and doctrine capable of protecting the region. Thus, the Eastern Caribbean (mini-states) Islands were specifically targeted along with the larger islands. Jamaica being a prime

TABLE 6.6 U.S. Military Assistance to the Carribean Basin, 1980-89[1] (in U.S.$ thousands)

	1980	1981	1982	1983	1984	1985	1986	1987	1988	1989
Caribbean										
Antigua-Barbuda	0	0	0	1,067	353	1,483	686	1,142	380	244
Barbados	30	30	56	55	70	192	344	642	89	961
Belize	0	0	20	48	204	919	612	410	325	288
Dominica	0	8	4	1,042	382	1,322	484	525	159	233
Dominican Republic	239	348	3,883	1,096	6,949	4,385	6,997	5,762	3,043	1,959
Grenada	0	0	0	0	2,335	3,450	464	557	625	80
Haiti	128	110	212	339	770	396	1,464	2,221	63	101
Jamaica	0	95	73	3,472	2,936	5,978	9,288	2,712	1,712	12,677
St. Kitts-Nevis	0	0	0	0	32	2,704	451	412	204	168
St. Lucia	0	2	8	1,065	410	225	429	348	136	236
St. Vincent	0	0	1	31	44	85	2,992	318	173	342
Trinidad-Tobago	0	15	0	5	0	39	50	78	70	11
Subtotal	397	608	4,257	8,220	14,116	21,178	24,261	15,027	6,979	17,300
Central America										
Costa Rica	0	31	46	4,084	2,430	14,825	6,787	1,123	1,650	563
El Salvador	2,535	35,412	66,248	69,032	121,598	139,754	130,551	109,779	109,221	87,002
Guatemala	10	4	0	71	2,669	984	3,911	4,239	10,067	15,354
Honduras	2,653	4,711	10,478	24,977	33,631	81,394	98,745	104,916	39,078	26,116
Panama	517	710	807	644	1,258	17,635	3,256	1,965	0	0
Subtotal	5,715	40,868	77,579	98,808	161,586	254,592	243,250	222,022	16,016	129,035
Total CBI	6,112	41,476	81,836	107,028	175,702	275,770	267,511	237,049	166,995	146,335

Source: U.S. Department of Defense, *Foreign Military Sales agreements, Foreign Military Construction Sales and Military Assistance Facts as of September 30, 1989* (Washington, D.C.: DOD, 1989).

1) Includes Foreign Military Sales agreements, Foreign Military Construction Sales agreements, Military Assistance Program, and International Military Education and Training Program.

targeted player in the policy, experienced a doubling of its military expenditures.

Confidential interviews with senior officers of the Jamaica Defense Force (JDF) revealed that at the time severe internal tensions developed among the officer corps due to their objections to U.S. inspired attempts to restructure the JDF (traditionally British in equipment, training, tactics and doctrine) along the lines of a U.S. oriented military force. Confidential sources also revealed that the debate over the issue of restructuring Jamaica's military led to a serious breakdown in relations between Prime Minister Seaga and the Chief of Staff of the JDF. Such has been the impact of the Reagan administration's policy of Caribbean militarization parallel with the CBI. Indeed, it appears that much more emphasis was placed on the military policy than making the CBI work. In conjunction with the policy pursued with respect to Jamaica, the United Sates also encouraged other Caribbean countries to substantially increase the strength and size of their military forces through arms purchases.

It is significant that along with the subsidized military sales agreements with the U.S. there were also commercial arms exports licensed under the U.S. Arms Export Control Act. U.S. Department of Defense records indicated that these sales increased from $1.2 million 1982 to a high (by Caribbean standards) of $5.6 million in 1986 (Deere et al, 1990). Analysts point to the impact the U.S. policy of militarization has had on the English speaking Caribbean, such as changing the role and status of the military from a relatively non-important entity to one of a much elevated status in countries that have relatively fragile political and economic systems. Indeed such a change could prove dangerous not only to the governments of some of these countries, but also to the very meaning of democracy itself. When one analyses the history of the Caribbean it becomes readily apparent that the process of militarization pursued by the Reagan administration in tandem with the CBI poses more a threat to the social and political structure of the region, than the region in general, or a particular country such as Cuba, poses to the United States. Most shocking is the realization that the Reagan administration's military policy ignored in the most blatant way, the essential developmental needs of the Caribbean and thus resulted in a substantial waste of the economic and other resources channeled to the area. This policy therefore, must be viewed as an obstacle to the economic and social development which as Deere et al, note is "crucial to the common security of the hemisphere" (Deere et al, 1990, p. 178).

The Caribbean Basin Initiative has not lived up to its vaunted expectations. Indeed, the rising level of expectation in the Caribbean Basin resulting from the high achievement and level of growth sold to the people of the region by the Reagan administration, has turned dangerously close to desperation, the outcome of which is hard to predict at this time.

As previously noted, at the time of the CBI's enactment in 1983 it was anticipated that Jamaica would be the "showcase" country among the CBI beneficiaries. However, as of mid-1991 it is apparent that the effect of the CBI on the economy of Jamaica--both the trade provisions and the developmental assistance--has been limited. Indeed, unless the policy is radically restructured the CBI will have no lasting positive impact on the value of Caribbean-U.S. trade. Further, the CBI will have contributed little if anything to the growth of Caribbean investment, employment, and living standards. The CBI, although not a total failure, has not begun to measure up to the expectations of proponents of the policy such as Prime Minister Edward Seaga and his U.S. counterpart President Ronald Reagan.

More than any other factors, several "entrenched" aspects of U.S. foreign policy toward the Third World and the Caribbean Basin are responsible for the CBI not measuring up to what was expected of it. First and foremost is the inherent contradiction in U.S. foreign policy between the expressed intention to promote democracy and objective of advancing free market/private enterprise policies of development.[25] Democracy and development in Third World countries come into conflict with U.S. foreign policy goals because they frequently "affect the U.S.'s self-defined security interests." What we observe is a self-fulfilling prophecy whereby policies such as the CBI do not work, thus forcing some governments to seek "radical" solutions to their social and economic problems, "which confirms to the U.S. that its security interests are indeed at stake. The frequent U.S. response—is to abandon the commitment to democracy." The events in Grenada in 1983 lend credence to this argument, and as Biddle and Stephens note, it is not a mistake but the manifestation of "an inherent feature of a policy which attempts to combine promotion of democracy with conservative, free market economic policies."[26]

A second important reason for the poor showing of the CBI is that the Reagan administration demonstrated very little if any political will in helping to make the initiative work. The most that was evident in terms of an effort by the administration was a carefully orchestrated publicity campaign aimed at selling to Congress and Caribbean governments the idea that the administration was serious about formulating and implementing a policy conducive to the economic and social developmental needs of the Caribbean Basin. In the case of Jamaica, elaborate publicity measures were undertaken, both by the Reagan administration and the Seaga government, to convince Jamaicans and especially supporters of Michael Manley's Peoples National Party (PNP) that adherence to a political and economic philosophy labeled "made in the U.S.A." and enthusiastically championed by Seaga and the Jamaica Labour Party (JLP), would bring tangible economic rewards to the country. The Reagan administration, however, did very little to influence politically the passage of the CBI bill through Congress.

A third and equally important reason for the poor showing of the CBI is the fact that from the outset the primary focus of the CBI was to assist private enterprise, particularly United States business interests, by ensuring that the Caribbean Basin is and remains open to and safe for foreign and to a lesser extent domestic private investments. Throughout the entire region country after country has reported the difficulties experienced by the indigenous business entrepreneur, in terms of production and marketing strategies and the availability of external financing.[27] In Jamaica the lucrative tourist industry is now virtually owned by foreign, mostly American, corporate interests. External economic factors have also adversely affected the trade performance of the CBI. In addition since most Caribbean Basin countries have their currencies pegged closely to the U.S. dollar's international exchange rate, they are usually unable to benefit from an export advantage when the dollar is strong. Also, the curtailment in multilateral lending by agencies such as the World Bank has retarded the growth and seriously affected the maintenance of export oriented infrastructure.

Finally, it appears that the CBI was doomed to a poor showing from the beginning in that a primary aim of the policy was to ensure the economic and military security of the United States by preserving its hegemonic control of the Caribbean Basin and the western hemisphere. Indeed, the Reagan administration's perceptions of the national security interests of the United States and the role the Caribbean and Central American region should play in that equation created an illusion in the minds of U.S. policy-makers as to the real significance of the area.[28] It is with this misconceived notion of the importance of the Caribbean Basin that the CBI was designed and thus is being implemented not only to protect the economic interests of U.S. investors in the Caribbean, but also to advance the political and military interests of the United States.

As noted earlier successive U.S. governments beginning with the Monroe adminisration in 1823, have viewed the Caribbean Basin region as a defensive perimeter vital to the security of the United States which must be protected at any cost. President Reagan's speech in February 1982 to the Organization of American States (OAS) announcing the CBI underscores that fact. The beliefs that form the foundation for Reagan's speech including the idea that the U.S. knows what is best for the rest of the hemisphere, and the conceptual framework underlining that idea might have been equally projected by Presidents Monroe in 1823, Theodore Roosevelt in 1904, Woodrow Wilson in 1916, Franklin D. Roosevelt in the 1930's and John Kennedy in 1961. Governments of the United States have for over two centuries exhibited an irrational fear of foreign political and economic ideologies entering the area. Likewise, the belief has been expressed that the entrance point of these ideologies would be through a Caribbean or Central American country. Because of this fear, U.S. policy toward this region has never been based on the interests or needs of the region, but rather on the greater strategic concerns of the U.S. The Caribbean Basin initiative is no exception.

Notes

1. Congressional Research Service, Issue Brief #1B82074 CBI, Jonathan Sanford, 1983.

2. Abraham Lowenthal "Misplaced Emphasis," *Foreign Policy* 47:114-38, Summer 1982, p. 115.

3. Heilodord Gonzales, "The Caribbean Basin Initiative: Toward a Permanent Dole," *Inter-American Economic Affairs*, 36:87-93, Summer 1982, p. 24.

4. White House, Office of the Press Secretary, Text of Message of the President to the Congress of the United States (March 17, 1982) P. 5.

5. Ibid, See also 1981 Hearings, supra note 1, at 153-160 (testimony of Bolton).

6. Jean G. Zorn and Harold Mayerson, "The Caribbean Basin Initiative: Windfall for the Private Sector," *Lawyer of the Americas* 14:523-556, p. 525, Winter 1983.

7. Richard Newfarmer, "Economic Policy Toward The Caribbean Basin: The Balance Sheet," *Journal of International Studies and World Affairs* 1: (February 1985), P. 63; Emilio Pantojas-Garcia, "The U.S. Caribbean Initiative and the Puerto Rican Experience: Some Parallels and Lessons," *Latin American Perspectives*, 12; 4:(1985), p. 105-127.

8. U.S. Department of Commerce, *1987 Guidebook: The Caribbean Basin Initiative* (Washington, D.C.: International Trade Administration, 1986.)

9. Anthony Payne "Creative Politics: Jamaica's Approach to Independence," *Caribbean Review*, Spring 1988 No. 1, Vol. XVI, p. 4-8 and 30-31.

10. Ibid

11. "Report on the Committee Delegation Mission to the Caribbean Basin and Recommendations to Improve the Effectiveness of the Caribbean Basin Initiative.", Subcommittee on Oversight Committee on Ways and Means, May 5, 1987, P. 22.

12. Ibid; *Christian Science Monitor*, March 19, 1987.

13. Report of a Congressional Study Mission and Symposium on the Caribbean Basin Initiative. Sept. 18-19, 1987. To the Committee on Foreign Affairs U.S. House of Representatives.

14. U.S. ITC, Operation of the Trade Agreements Program, 39th. Report, 1987 (Washington, D.C.: USITC, 1988).

15. U.S. ITC, Impact of the CBERA, Fourth Report, 1988, P. 1-9, Note 23.

16. USITC, Operation of Trade Agreements Program, P. 5-18, and USITC, Impact of CBERA, Fourth Report, 1988, P. 1-9 and Table 1-9.

17. See Direction of Trade Statistics Yearbook (Jamaica), see also the Europa Year Book 1988, Introductory Survey (Jamaica).

18. Ibid.

19. For an examination of the 936 Funding Program, see the 1989 Guidebook: Caribbean Basin Initiative, U.S. Dept. of Commerce. International Trade Administration U.S. and Foreign Commercial Service. Washington, D.C.

20. Jamaica: Financial Report, 1984, 1985, 1986. Prepared by Samuel Montagu and Co., Limited, for the government of Jamaica.

21. See Haar, Jerry. The Caribbean Basin Initiative: An Interim Assessment of the Trade Provision's Impact. Florida International University, Miami.

22. George D. Moffett III, "Despite Reagan Initiative, Caribbean Basin Trade Woes Worsen," *Christian Science Monitor*, March 19, 1987.

23. Ibid.

24. Report on "The Committee Delegation Mission to the Caribbean Basin and Recommendations to Improve the Effectiveness of the CBI:" Subcommittee on Oversight of the Committee on Ways and Means U.S. House of Representatives 1987.

25. For an anaylsis of dependent development and foreign policy see, William J. Biddle and John D. Stephens, "Dependent Development and Foreign Policy: The Case of Jamaica." International Studies Quarterly, Vol .33, No. 4, December 1989, p. 411-434.

26. Ibid, p. 430.

27. Peter Johnson, "The Caribbean Basin Initiative: A Positive Departure," *Foreign Policy* 47:115-122 (1982).

28. See "The Caribbean Basin and Global Security: Strategic Implications of the Soviet Threat." CAUSA International 1985.

Bibliography

Books

Adelman, Alan, and Reid Reading, eds. *Confrontation in the Caribbean Basin.* University of Pittsburgh: Center for Latin American Studies, University Center for International Studies, 1984.

Adkin, Mark. *Urgent Fury: The Battle for Grenada* Lexington, MA: Lexington Books, D.C. Heath and Company, 1989.

Ambursley, Fitzroy, and Robin Cohen, eds. *Crisis in the Caribbean.* New York: Monthly Review Press, 1983.

Anderson, Thomas D. *Geopolitics of the Caribbean.* New York: Praeger Publishers, 1984.

Andic, Fuat, Suphan Andic, and Douglas Dosser. *A Theory of Economic Integration For Developing Countries.* London: George Allen and Unwin, Ltd., 1971.

Atlantic Council's Working Group on the Caribbean. *Western Interests and U.S. Policy Options in the Caribbean Basin.* Boston: Oelgeschlager, Gunn & Hain, Publishers, Inc., 1984.

Bell, Wendell. Jamaican Leaders: *Political Attitudes in a New Nation.* Berkley: University of California Press, 1964.

Bell, Wendell, ed. *The Democratic Revolution in the West Indies.* Cambridge: Schenkman Publishing Company, Inc., 1967.

Bishop, Maurice. *In Nobody's Backyard: Maurice Bishop's Speeches: 1979-1983.* Edited by Chris Searle with introduction by Richard Hart. London: Zed Books, Ltd., 1984.

Black, Clinton V. *Jamaica Guide.* Jamaica: William Collins & Sangster (Jamaica) Ltd., 1973.

Blasier, Cole. *The Hovering Giant: U.S. Responses to Revolutionary Change in Latin America.* Pittsburgh: University of Pittsburgh Press, 1976.

Coleman, Kenneth M., and George C. Herring, eds. *The Central American Crises*. Wilmington: Scholarly Resources Inc., 1985.

Cortada, James N., and James W. Cortada. *U.S. Foreign Policy In The Caribbean, Cuba, And Central America*. New York: Praeger Publishers, 1985.

Cronon, David E. *Marcus Garvey*. Madison: The University of Wisconsin Press, 1969.

Cumper, G. E. *The Economy Of the West Indies*. Connecticut: Greenwood Press, 1974.

Dealy, Glen Caudill. *An Honorable Peace in Central America*. Belmont: Brooks/Cole Publishing Company, 1988.

Deere, Carmen Diana, Peggy Antrobus, Lynn Bolles, Edwin Melendez, Peter Phillips, Marcia Rivera, and Helen Safa. *In the Shadows of the Sun*. Boulder: Westview Press, 1990.

Dunn, Peter M., and Bruce W. Watson, eds. *American Intervention in Grenada: The Implications of Operation "Urgent Fury."* Boulder: Westview Press, 1985.

Eisner, G. *Jamaica 1830-1930 A Study in Economic Growth*. Manchester: Manchester University Press, 1961.

Erisman, H. Michael, and John D. Martz, eds. *Colossus Challenged: The Struggle for Caribbean Influence*. Boulder: Westview Press, 1982.

Falcoff, Mark, Wiarda Falcoff, Howard J. Falcoff, with Ernest Evans, Jiri Valenta, and Virginia Valenta. *The Communist Challenge in the Caribbean and Central America*. Washington: American Enterprise Institute for Public Policy Research, 1987.

Fauriol, Georges A. *Foreign Policy Behavior of Caribbean State*. Lanham & London: University Press of America, 1984.

Feinberg, Richard E. *The Intemperate Zone*. New York: W.W. Norton & Company, 1983.

Forbes, John D. *Jamaica*. Washington: American Enterprise Institute for Public Policy Reseaerch, 1985.

Gayle, Dennis John. *The Small Developing State*. Hampshire, England: Gower Publishing Company, 1986.

Girvan, Norman. *Corporate Imperialism: Conflict and Exproriation*. White Plains: M.E. Sharpe, Inc., 1976.

Guess, George M. *The Politics of United States Foreign Aid*. London: Croom Helm, LTD., 1987.

Haig, Alexander M., Jr. *Caveat: Realism, Reagan, and Foreign Policy*. New

York: Macmillan Publishing Company, 1984.
Hayter, Teresa. *Aid As Imperialism.* England: Penguin Books, 1971.
Hurwitz, Samuel J., and Edith F. Hurwitz. *Jamaica: A Historical Portrait.* New York: Praeger Publishers, Inc., 1971.
Katz, Mark N. *Gorbachev's Military Policy in the Third World.* Foreword by William E. Odom. The Washington Papers, no. 140. New York: Praeger Publishers with The Center for Strategic and International Studies, 1989.
Knight, Franklin W. *The Caribbean.* New York: Oxford University Press, 1978.
Kolko, Gabriel. *Confronting the Third World.* New York: Patheon Books, 1988.
Langley, Lester D. *Central America: The Real Stakes.* Chicago: The Dorsey Press, 1985.
_____. *The United States and the Caribbean, 1900-1970.* 1980. Rpt. as The United States and the Caribbean in the Twentieth Century. Athens, Georgia: The University of Georgia Press, 1985.
_____. *The Banana Wars.* Chicago: The Dorsey Press, 1988.
Levine, Barry B., ed. *The New Cuban Presence in The Caribbean.* Boulder: Westview Press, 1983.
Lewis, Gordon K. Grenada: *The Jewel Despoiled.* Baltimore: The Johns Hopkins University Press, 1987.
Maingot, Anthony P. "The Caribbean: The Structure of Modern-Conservative Societies." In *Latin America, Its Problems and its Promise: A Multi-Disciplinary Introduction,* pp. 362-378. Edited by Jan Knippers Black. Boulder: Westview Press, 1989.
Mandle, Jay R. *Big Revolution, Small Country: The Rise and Fall of the Grenada Revolution.* Lanham, Maryland: The North-South Publishing Company, Inc., 1985.
Manley, Michael. *The Politics of Change: A Jamaican Testament.* Great Britain: Andre' Deutsch Limited, 1974; reprint ed., Washington, D.C.: Howard University Press, 1975.
Manley, Norman Washington. *Norman Washington Manley and the New Jamaica: Selected Speeches and Writings 1938-68.* Edited with notes and introduction by Rex Nettleford. Trinidad and Jamaica: Longman Caribbean Limited, 1971.
Manley, Michael. Jamaica: *Struggle in the Periphery.* London: Third World Media, Howard Limited, 1982.
Marable, Manning. *African and Caribbean Politics.* London: Verso, 1987.

Martin, John Bartlow. *U.S. Policy in the Caribbean.* Boulder: Westview Press, 1978.

Martin, Tony, ed. *In Nobody's Backyard: The Grenada Revolution in its Own Words. Vol. I, The Revolution at Home.* Dover, Massachusetts: The Majority Press, 1983.

_____. *In Nobody's Backyard: The Grenada Revolution in its Own Words. Vol. II, Facing the World.* With the assistance of Dessima Williams. Dover, Massachusetts: The Majority Press, 1985.

Mathews, T.G., and F.M. Andic, eds. *Politics and Economics in the Caribbean.* Rio Piedras, Puerto Rico: Institute of Caribbean Studies, 1971.

McDonald, Vincent R., ed. *The Caribbean Economics.* New York: MSS Information Corp., 1972.

Migdal, Joel S. *Strong Societies and Weak States.* Princeton: Princeton University Press, 1988.

Moran, Fernando, Irving Kristol, Michial D. Barnes, Alois Mertes, and Daniel Oduber. *Third World Instability: Central America.* New York: Council on Foreign Relations, Inc., 1985.

Mordecai, John. *The West Indies.* Evanston: Northwestern University Press, 1968.

Needler, Martin C. *An Introduction to Latin American Politics: The Structure of Conflict.* 2nd ed. Englewood Cliffs, New Jersey: Prentice-Hall, Inc., 1983.

Nettleford, Rex M. *Mirror Mirror.* 1970. Rpt. as Identity, Race and Protest in Jamaica. New York: William Morrow & Company, Inc., 1972.

Palmer, Ransford W. *Problems of Development in Beautiful Countries.* Maryland: North-South Publishing, 1984.

Parenti, Michael. *The Sword and The Dollar.* New York: St. Martin's Press, 1989.

Payne, Anthony. *The International Crisis in the Caribbean.* Baltimore: The Johns Hopkins University Press, 1984.

_____. *The Politics of the Caribbean Community 1961-79.* New York: St. Martin's Press, 1980.

_____. *Politics in Jamaica.* London: C. Hurst & Company, 1988.

Payne, Anthony, Paul Sutton, and Tony Thorndike. *Grenada: Revolution and Invasion.* New York: St. Martin's Press, 1984.

Rourke, John T. *Making Foreign Policy: United States, Soviet Union, China.* Pacific Grove, California: Brooks/Cole Publishing Company, a Division of Wadsworth, Inc., 1990.

Scott, Harriet Fast, and William F. Scott. *Soviet Military Doctrine.* Boulder: Westview Press, 1988.

Seabury, Paul, and Walter A. McDougall, eds. *The Grenada Papers.* Foreword by Sidney Hook. San Francisco: Institute for Contemporary Studies Press, 1984.

Searle, Chris, ed. *In Nobody's Backyard.* London: Zed Books, Ltd., 1984.

Sherlock, Philip. *Keeping Company with Jamaica.* London: Macmillan Publishers, 1984.

Skidmore, Thomas E. and Peter H. Smith. *Modern Latin America.* 2nd ed. New York: Oxford University Press, 1989.

Stephens, Evelyne Huber, and John D. Stephens. *Jamaica's Democratic Socialist Experience.* Washington: The Woodrow Wilson International Center for Scholars, 1985.

_____. *Democratic Socialism in Jamaica.* New Jersey: Princeton University Press, 1986.

Stone, Carl. *Class, State, and Democracy in Jamaica.* New York: Praeger Publishers, 1986.

_____. *Democracy and Clientelism in Jamaica.* New Brunswick: Transaction Books, 1980.

_____. *Politics Versus Economics: The 1989 Election in Jamaica.* Kingston, Jamaica: Heinemann Publishers (Caribbean) Limited, 1989.

_____. *Power in the Caribbean Basin.* Philadelphia: Institute for the Study of Human Issues, 1986.

Stone, Carl, and Paget Henry, eds. *The Newer Caribbean.* Philadelphia: Institute for the Study of Human Issues, 1983.

Thomas, Ann Van Wynen, and A.J. Thomas, Jr. *The Organization of American States.* Dallas: Southern Methodist University Press, 1963.

Thompson, Loren B. *Low-Intensity Conflict: The Pattern of Warfare in the Modern World.* The Georgetown International Security Studies Series. Lexington, Massachusetts: Lexington Books, D.C. Heath and Company, 1989.

Urquhart, Brian. *Decolonization and World Peace.* Austin: University of Texas Press, 1989.

Valenta, Juri, and Herbert J. Ellison, eds. *Grenada and Soviet/Cuban Policy.* Boulder: Westview Press, 1986.

Wagner, Geoffrey. Red Calypso. Washington, D.C.: Regnery Gateway Inc., 1988.

Weigel, George. *American Interests, American Purpose: Moral Reasoning and U.S. Foreign Policy.* Foreword by Max M. Kampelman. The Washington Papers, no. 139. New York: Praeger Publishers with The Center for Strategic and International Studies, 1989.

White, Richard Alan. *The Morass.* New York: Harper & Row, 1984.

Wiarda, Howard J., and Harvey F. Kline, eds. *Latin American Politics & Development.* Boston: Houghton Mifflin Company, 1979.

Wiarda, Howard J., and Mark Falcoff with Ernest Evans and Jiri and Virginia Valenta. *The Communist Challenge in the Caribbean and Central America.* Washington, D.C.: American Enterprise Institute for Public Policy Research, 1987.

Young, Alma H., and Dion E. Phillips. *Militarization in the Non-Hispanic Caribbean.* Boulder: Lynne Rienner Publishers, Inc., 1986.

Journal Articles

Alexander, Gerald. "The Calypso Blues: Why the Caribbean Initiative Isn't Working." *Policy Review* 38 (Fall 1986): 55-59.

Armstrong, Adrienne. "The Political Consequences of Economic Dependence." *Journal of Conflict Resolution* 25, no. 3 (September 1981): 401-428.

Axline, W. Andrew. "Political Change and U.S. Strategic Concerns in the Caribbean." *Latin American Research Review* 13, no. 2 (1988): 214-225.

Biddle, William Jesse, and John D. Stephens. "Dependent Development and Foreign Policy: The Case of Jamaica." *International Studies* Quarterly 33, no. 4 (December 1989): 411-434.

Braveboy-Wagner, Jacquelin Anne. Caribbean Foreign Policy: An Examination of Its Limitations and Needs." *Caribbean Affairs* 1, no. 3 (July-September 1988): 77-89.

Chaney, Elsa M. "Scenarios of Hunger in the Caribbean: Migration, Decline of Smallholder Agriculture, and the Femininization of Farming." *International Studies Notes* 14, no. 3 (Fall 1989): 67-71.

Corrada, Baltasar. "The Caribbean Basin Initiative: Puerto Rico Will Benefit." *Foreign Policy* 47 (Summer 1982): 126-128.

Fauriol, Georges A. "The Shadow of Latin American Affairs." *Foreign Affairs: America and the World* 1989/90.

Feinberg, Richard E., Richard Newfarmer, and Bernadette Orr. "The Battle Over the CBI." *Caribbean Review.*

Feinberg, Richard E. "Central America: No Easy Answers." *Foreign Affairs* (Summer 1981): 1021-1146.

Feinberg, Richard E., and Richard S. Newfarmer. "The Caribbean Basin Initiative: A Bilateralist Gamble." *Foreign Policy* 47 (Summer 1982): 133-138.

Foreign Affairs: America and the World 1988/89 68, no. 1 (1989).

Gonzalez, Heliodoro. "The Caribbean Basin Initiative: Toward a Permanent Dole." *Inter-American Economic Affairs* 36 (Summer 1982): 87-93.

Gunn, Gillian. "Will Castro Fall?" *Foreign Policy* 79 (Summer 1990): 132-150.

Hernandez-Colon, Rafael. "The Caribbean Basin Initiative: Puerto Rico Partner or Victim." *Foreign Policy* 47 (Summer 1982): 123-125.

"Jamaica." Latin American and Caribbean Review (1980): 215-218.

James, Canute. "Jamaica." *Latin American and Caribbean Review* (1985): 209-212.

Johnson, Peter "The Caribbean Basin Initiative: A Positive Departure." *Foreign Policy* 47 (Summer 1982): 118-122. Latin American Perspectives 17, no. 1 (Winter 1990).

Lowenthal, Abraham F. "Rediscovering Latin America." *Foreign Affairs* (Fall 1990): 27-41.

_____. "The Caribbean Basin Initiative: Misplaced mphasis." *Foreign Policy* 47 (Summer 1982): 114-118.

Manley, Michael. "Overcoming Insularity in Jamaica." *Foreign Affairs* 49, no. 1 (October 1970): 100-110.

_____. "Southern Needs." *Foreign Policy* 80 (Fall 1990): 40-55.

Manning, Robert. "Caribbean Circle of Crisis." South (London) 4 (January-February 1981): 21-27.

O'Flaherty, J. Daniel. "Finding Jamaica's Way." *Foreign Policy* 31 (Summer 1978): 137-158.

Pantojas-Garcia, Emilio. "The U.S. Caribbean Basin Initiative and the Puerto Rican Experience." *Latin American Perspectives* 12 (Fall 1985): 105-128.

Pastor, Robert. "Sinking in the Caribbean Basin." *Foreign Affairs* 60 (Summer 1982): 1038-1058.

Payne, Anthon John. "Creative Politics: Jamaica's Approach to Independence." *Caribbean Review* 16, no. 1 (Spring 1988): 4-31.

Purcell, Susan Kaufman. "Cuba's Cloudy Future." *Foreign Affairs* (Summer 1990): 114-130.

Stone, Carl. "Does Jamaica Have the Political Skills for Crisis Management? Or, Is this Just a Ceasefire?" *Caribbean Affairs* 1, no. 3 (July-September

1988): 137-150.

"Struggle for the Caribbean." *Latin American and Caribbean Review* (1981-82): 15-20.

Watson, Hilbourne A. "The Caribbean Basin Initiative and Caribbean Development: A Critical Analysis." *Contemporary Marxism* 10 (1985): 1-37.

Weintraub, Sidney. "The Caribbean Basin Initiative: A Flawed Model." Foreign Policy 47 (Summer 1982): 128-133.

Zorn, Jean G., and Harold Mayerson. "The Caribbean Basin Initiative: A windfall for the Private Sector." *Lawyer of the Americas* 14 (Winter 1983): 523-556.

Newspapers

"Caribbean Officials Criticize Outside Pressure on Panama." *New York Times*, 23 May 1988.

"3 Caribbean Premiers Defend Reagan's Development Plan." *New York Times*, 18 June 1982.

"CBI Delay Likely." *Jamaica Weekly Gleaner*, 23 May 1988.

Crossette, Barbara. "Caribbean Views Plan as 'Bold' But Not a 'Miracle.'" *New York Times*, 25 February 1982.

Farnsworth, Clyde H. "The 'Good Neighbor' Offers Little Aid, Less Trade." *Miami Herald*, 1 February 1988.

French, Howard W. "Jamaican Leader to Meet Bush Today." *New York Times*, 3 May 1990, sec. A, p. 7.

_____. "Shifts in U.S. Policy Sought to Spur Caribbean Trade." *New York Times*, 1 March 1990, sec. C, pp. 1+.

Gwertzman, Bernard. "Mitterrand, in U.S., Backs Caribbean Recovery Project." *New York Times*, 13 March 1982, p. 3.

_____. "Reagan Announces Aid for Caribbean and Assails Cuba." *New York Times*, 25 February 1982, sec. A, pp.1+.

Jacobsen, Herbert L. "False Promises of the Caribbean Basin Initiative." *Wall Street Journal*, 4 April 1986, p. 21.

Kaslow, Amy. "U.S. Rethinking Caribbea Trade."*Christian Science Monitor*, 28 March 1990, p. 8.

Manchester Trade, 8 September 1989, 11 September 1989, and 25 September 1989.

Moffett, George D. III. "Despite Reagan Initiative, Caribbean Basin Trade

Woes Worsen." *Christian Science Monitor,* 19 March 1987, p. 5+.
Pastor, Robert. "Central America Commission Requires Freedom, Clear Goal." *Louisville Times,* 28 July 1983.
Street, James H. "A 'Basin' Marshall Plan." New York Times, 3, 1982.
Weiss, Julian M. "Trade Bill Could Reverse Economic Progress in the Caribbean." *Christian Science Monitor,* 13 August 1987, p. 10.
Autin, John. "A New Orleans Matchmaker Conference Sets Pace for Central American Trade." *Business America* (18 July 1980): 13.
"Address to Organization of American States." *Congressional Quarterly* (27 February 1982): 491-493.
"Barbados: Economy Relies on U.S. for Products, Investment." *Business America* (1 August 1988): 25.
"The Caribbean." *Economist* (6 August 1988): 3-18.
"The Caribbean: Corporate Misgivings About U.S. Aid Plans." *Business Week* (5 April 1982): 40-41.
Congressional Digest 62 (March 1983): 69-96.
Council on Hemispheric Affairs. *Washington Report on the Hemisphere* 6, no. 10 (February 1986).
_____. *Washington Report on the Hemisphere* 11, no. 4 (14 November 1990).
_____. *Washington Report on the Hemisphere* 11, no. 8 (23 January 1991).
Donnelly, Harrison. "Senate Seeks to Restore Reagan Funding Requests to New Supplemental Bill." *Congressional Quarterly* (7 August 1982): 1882.
Economist: A Survey of the Caribbean 6 August 1988.
Felton, John. "Caribbean Basin Proposal Faces Lengthy Hearings; Numerous Objections Cited." *Congressional Quarterly* (27 March 1982): 681-684.
"Grant Will Expand Minority Opportunities in Caribbean Basin." *Business America* (21 July 1986): 15.
Greenwald, John. "Experimenting Under the Sun." *Time,* 24 May 1982.
"Jamaica: Going to Pot." *Economist,* 7 May 1988, p. 37-38.
Klotzbach, Thomas. "Caribbean Basin: Trade Expansion Comes With Economic Progress." *Business America* 109, no. 9 (25 April 1988): 42-43.
Latin American Regional Reports Caribbean 22 January 1987, 27 August 1987, 25 February 1988.
Lindorff, Dave. "Grenadian Menace." *The Nation* 236, no. 15 (16 April 1983): 466-467.
Massaquoi, Hans J. "Interview with Jamaica Prime Minister Michael Manley." *Ebony* (February 1990): 110+.
Massing, Michael. "Unlikely Cold War Hot Spot." *Nation* (14 May 1983):

604-606.

"Message on Caribbean Basin." *Congressional Quarterly* (27 March 1982): 706-708.

Millett, Richard. "THe United States and Latin America." *Current History* 83, no. 490 (February 1984): 49-85.

Murray, Alan. "House Eases Trade Barriers to Some Caribbean Imports." *Congressional Quarterly* (16 July 1983): 1466.

Plattner, Andy. "Another Supplemental Faces Possible Veto." *Congressional Quarterly* (14 August 1982): 1951-1952.

"Reagan's Blueprint." *U.S. News & World Report*, 8 March 1982, pp. 20-23.

"The Reagan 'Caribbean Basin Initiative.'" *Congressional Digest* 62 (March 1983): 69-96.

Segal, Aaron. "Caribbean Realities." *Current History* (March 1985): 127-135.

Tadeu, Americo A. "Caribbean Basin: Economies Are Expected to Grow Modestly in '87." *Business America* 10, no. 20 (28 September 1987): 35.

Tadeu, Americo A., and Thomas Wilde. "Twin Caribbean Islands Invite Tourism Investment." *Business America* (5 December 1988): 22-23.

"Trade Show is Part of Effort to Open U.S. Market to Caribbean Apparel." *Business America* 109, no. 6 (14 March 1988): 16.

Whittle, Richard. "Caribbean Aid Blocked on House Floor." *Congressional Quarterly* (31 July 1982): 1866.

_____. "Caribbean Aid Given Last Chance for 1982." *Congressional Quarterly* (14 August 1982): 1957-1958.

_____. "El Salvador, Latin America May Move to Center Stage in Debate on Foreign Aid." *Congressional Quarterly* (10 April 1982): 803-804.

_____. "Reagan Revives Subsidized Arms Aid Plan." *Congressional Quarterly* (6 March 1982): 512.

_____. "Reagan Wins First Success on Caribbean Plan." *Congressional Quarterly* (24 July 1982): 1770-1771.

_____. "Schultz, Regan Urge Senate Finance Panel to Act Quickly on CBI." *Congressional Quarterly* (7 August 1982): 1899.

_____. "World Bank Official Rejects Special Fund." *Congressional Quarterly* (10 July 1982): 1653.

"Why Jamaica's Economy May Run Aground." *Business Week* (18 October 1982): 162-163.

Wylie, Scott. "Caribbean Basin Initiative: One Year Later." *Business America* (7 January 1985): 2-15.

Yearbooks and Annuals

The Europa Yearbook 1988. 1505-1511.
Kruzel, Joseph, ed. 1989-90 *American Defense Annual.* Lexington, Massachusetts and Toronto: Mershon Center, Ohio State University and Lexington Books, D.C. Heath and Company, 1989.

Published Papers

Gayle, Dennis John. *Trade Issues in the Anglophone Caribbean.* Edited by Richard Tardanico. Miami: Latin American and Caribbean Center and the Florida-Caribbean Institute, Florida International University, 1989.

Unpublished Papers

Haar, Jerry. "The Caribbean Basin Initiative: An Interim Assessment of the Trade Provision's Impact." Florida International University.
Hewan, Clinton G. "The Caribbean Basin Initiative: Impact on Trade Between Jamaica and the United States." 1988.
Hewan, Clinton G. "Politics and International Relations of the Independent West Indian Islands: Jamaica, Trinidad and Tobago, Barbados; From Colonialism to Independence." Masters Thesis, University of Cincinnati, 1971.
Lewis, Patrick A. "The Riots in the British West Indies, 1935-1938: The Causes and the Aftermath." Masters Thesis, University of Cincinnati, 1968.
McElroy, Jerome L. and Klaus de Albuquerque. "Sustainable Small-Scale Agriculture in Small Caribbean Islands." Paper prepared for the Midwest Association of Latin American Studies Meeting in Cincinnati, Ohio, 12-13 October 1990.
Wilson, Bruce M. "Neo-Liberals, Social Democrats, and Economic Crises: The Cases of Costa Rica and Jamaica." Paper prepared for the Midwest Association of Latin American Studies Meeting in Cincinnati, Ohio, 12-13 October 1990.

Documents

CARICOM (Caribbean Community). Secretariat. *Trade Performance Under*

the Caribbean Basin Initiative. WP(CBI) 88/1/3, 1988.
CARICOM (Caribbean Community). Secretariat. *Review of the Caribbean Basin Initiative (CBI).* CCM 88/32/16, 1988.
International Security Council, a project of CAUSA International. *The Caribbean Basin and Global Security: Strategic Implications of the Soviet Threat.* 1985.
Jamaica. *Budget Debate Speech by Hon. Michael Manley, Prime Minister of Jamaica,* 2 May 1973.
Jamaica. *Budget Debate Speech by Hon. Michael Manley, Prime Minister of Jamaica,* 29 May 1974.
Jamaica. *Budget Debate Speech by Hon. Michael Manley, Prime Minister of Jamaica,* 27 May 1975.
Jamaica. *Caribbean Free Trade Association Agreement and Related Documents.*
Jamaica. *A Development Plan for the Caribbean.* Address to the CARICOM Foreign Ministers of Jamaica by the Prime Minister the Rt. Hon. Edward Seaga, 4 September 1981.
Jamaica. House of Representatives. *The Jamaica (Constitution) Order in Council 1962.* 1962 No. 1550. Caribbean and North Atlantic Territories.
Jamaica. House of Representatives. *Jamaica Gazette: Supplement Proclamations, Rules and Regulations.* Supplement to the Jamaica (Constitution) Order in Council 1962 No. 1550 Caribbean and North Atlantic Territories.
Jamaica. *Jamaica: Financial Report.* September 1984.
Jamaica. National Planning Agency. *Economic and Social Survey Jamaica* 1975.
Jamaica. National Planning Agency. *Economic and Social Survey Jamaica* 1976.
Jamaica. People's National Party. *Democratic Socialism: The Jamaican Model.* Kingston: People's National Party.
Jamaica. People's National Party. *The 1980 Election Manifesto of the People's National Party.* Kingston: People's National Party.
Jamaica. People's National Party. *Principles and Objectives.* Kingston: Golden Printing Service.
Jamaica. *Report of Meeting Between Embassy Group and Friends of the Caribbean Staff Members.*
Jamaica. *A Review of the Performance of the Jamaican Economy: 1981-1983.*
Jamaica. *Treaty Establishing the Caribbean Community.* Appendix B.
SELA (Sistema Economico Latinoamericano). Permanent Secretariat. *The Caribbean Basin Initiative: Current Situation and Outlook.* SP/CL/XIV.O/Di No. 2, 1988.
U.S. Congress. House. *A Bill to Promote Economic Revitalization and*

Facilitate Expansion of Economic Opportunities in the Caribbean Basin Region on H.R. 2769, 98th Cong., 1st sess., 1983.
U.S. Congress. House. *Report on the Congressional Mission Study Missions and Consultation on the U.S. House of Representatives.* Bill HR3101 to Improve the Operation of the Caribbean Basin Economic Recovery Act of 1987 and a Draft Bill Entitled The Caribbean Community Development Act of 1988.
U.S. Congress. House. Committee on Foreign Affairs. *The Caribbean Basin Initiative: Hearings and Markup: Hearing before the Subcommittees on International Economic Policy and Trade and Inter-American Affairs on H.R. 5900,* 97th Cong., 2nd sess., 1982.
U.S. Congress. House. Committee on Foreign Affairs. *The Caribbean Basin Initiative and U.S. Minority Participation.* Hearing before the Subcommittees on International Economic Policy and Trade and on Western Hemisphere Affairs of the House Committee on Foreign Affairs. 99th Cong., 1st sess., 1985.
U.S. Congress. House. Committee on Foreign Affairs. *The Caribbean Basin Initiative: Caribbean Views.* Report of a Congressional Study Mission and Symposium on the Caribbean Basin Initiative to the House Committee on Foreign Affairs. 1987.
U.S. Congress. House. Committee on Foreign Affairs. *The Caribbean Basin Initiative: A Congressional Study Mission and Symposium.* Hearings before the Subcommittees on International Economic Policy and Trade and on Western Hemisphere Affairs of the House Committee on Foreign Affairs. 100th Cong., 1st sess., 1987.
U.S. Congress. House. Committee on Ways and Means. *Review of the Impact and Effectiveness of the Casribbean Basin Initiative.* Hearings Before the Subcommittee on Oversight of the House Committee on Ways and Means. Serial 99-70, 99th Cong., 2nd sess., 1986.
U.S. Congress. House. Committee on Ways and Means. *Report on the Committee Delegation Mission to the Caribbean Basin and Recommendations to IMprove the Effectiveness of the Caribbean Basin Initiative.* 100th Cong., 1st sess., 1987.
U.S. Congress. House. Committee on Ways and Means. Testimony of Ambassador Clayton Yeutter, United States Trade Representative, before the Subcommittee on Trade of the Committee on Ways and Means on Enhancement of the Caribbean Basin Economic Recovery Act. 1988.
U.S. Congress. Senate. Senator Dole speaking for the Bill to Promote

Expansion Revitalization and Facilitate Expansion of Economic Opportunity in the Caribbean Basin Region. S. Res. 2237, 98th Cong., 1st sess., 18 March 1982. Congressional Record.

U.S. Congressional Research Service. The Library of Congress. IB82074, 1982.

U.S. Department of Commerce. International Trade Administration. *Foreign Economic Trends and Their Implications for the United States.* 1987.

U.S. Department of Commerce. International Trade Administration. *Caribbean and Central American Export Performance 1980-1987.* 1988.

U.S. Department of Commerce. International Trade Administration. *Caribbean Basin Investment Survey.* 1988.

U.S. Department of Commerce. International Trade Administration. *Caribbean Basin Initiative.* 1989 Guidebook. 1988.

U.S. Department of Commerce. International Trade Administration. *CBI Business Bulletin*, vol. VII, no. 2, 1990.

U.S. Department of State. Bureau of Public Affairs. *GIST: Caribbean Basin Initiative.* 1982.

U.S. Department of State. *Caribbean Basin Initiative Reviewed by Foreign Ministers.* 1982.

U.S. Department of State. Bureau of Public Affairs. *GIST: U.S. Interests in the Caribbean Basin.* May 1982.

U.S. Department of State. Bureau of Public Affairs. *Caribbean Basin Initiative.* Current Policy No. 370 (1982).

U.S. Department of State. Bureau of Public Affairs. *U.S. Approach to Problems i the Caribbean Basin.* Current Policy No. 412 (1982).

U.S. Department of State. Bureau of Public Affairs. *Programs Underway for the Caribbean Basin Initiative.* Current Policy No. 442 (1982).

U.S. Department of State. Bureau of Public Affairs. *Background on the Caribbean Basin Initiative.* Special Report No. 97 (1982).

U.S. Department of State. Bureau of Public Affairs. *CBI and the U.S. National Interest.* Current Policy No. 799 (1986).

U.S. Department of State. Bureau of Public Affairs. *The CBI: Important Incentives for Trade and Investment.* Current Policy No. 1965 (1988).

U.S. Department of State. Bureau of Public Affairs. Five Years of the Caribbean Basin Initiative. Current Policy No. 1241 (1989).

U.S. Department of State and the Department of Defense. *Grenada Documents: An Overview and Selection.* 1984.

U.S. General Accounting Office. *Caribbean Basin Initiative: Need for More Reliable Data on Business Activity Resulting From the Initiative.* Briefing

Report to the Chairman, Subcommittee on Oversight, Committee on Ways and Means, House of Representatives. GAO/NSIAD-86-201BR, 1986.

U.S. General Accounting Office. Caribbean Basin Initiative: *Impact on Selected Countries*. Report to the Chairman, Subcommittee on Western Hemisphere and Peace Corps Affairs, Committee on Foreign Relations, U.S. Senate. GAO/NSIAD-88-177, 1988.